D1481801

PENGUIN AFRICAN LIBRARY AP13

Edited by Ronald Segal

Which Way Africa?

BASIL DAVIDSON

MONTREAT-ANDERSON
COLLEGE LIBRARY

BASIL DAVIDSON

Which Way Africa?

The Search for a New Society

Penguin Books
Baltimore / Maryland

Penguin Books Ltd, Harmondsworth, Middlesex, England
Penguin Books Inc., 3300 Clipper Mill Road, Baltimore 11, Md, U.S.A.
Penguin Books Pty Ltd, Ringwood,
Victoria, Australia

First published 1964

Copyright © Basil Davidson 1964

Made and printed in Great Britain by C. Nicholls & Company Ltd
Set in Monotype Plantin

This book is sold subject to the condition that it shall not, by way of trade,
be lent, re-sold, hired out, or otherwise disposed of without the
publisher's consent, in any form of binding or cover other than that
in which it is published

It is now such a time that every man stands under the eaves of his own hat, and sings what he pleases.

Ben Jonson

Contents

1 A Time of Great Change

There are brief climactic periods in human history, maybe a few weeks or months or as long as several years, when the destiny of whole peoples seems to resolve itself for better or for worse. The old gives way to the new; and the new goes forward with a force that is sudden and mysterious.

Afterwards, peering back into moods and memories, historians explain this suddenness and mystery as an illusion, as the mere surface shift from deep-down currents of social and collective change. But those who were there at the time, who watched or played a part themselves, are none the less likely to recall their wonder and delight – or, according to their condition, their trouble and dismay – as though these emotions had really been the product of a kind of miracle. This is how it appears to have happened to people at all times of great upheaval. And this is undoubtedly how it has happened to millions of people in Africa these past few years.

Ten or fifteen years ago no more than a few skilful prophets and romantics could have believed that the year 1963 would produce a meeting of thirty-two independent African states, all but two of them former colonies. The rate of emancipation might be rapid: surely it could not be as rapid as that? And yet it was.

But even if the suddenness and mystery are an illusion, concealing the long and deep growth of a new independence, the present fact of *change*, and therefore the present fact of *choice*, are pressingly real. Africa today may be in many ways remarkably the same as it was ten years ago: given the general groundwork of technological poverty, nothing else could be expected. Potentially, though, everything of importance in Africa has changed; and it has done so in a sense that may be called revolutionary. It has changed so far that everything now seems possible where little or nothing seemed possible before. And people of the most various kinds and loyalties up and down the continent, from the peasants of war-shattered Algeria in the far north to the harried populations of the distant south, and all the way between, are now confronted with the central questions of a great and often passionate debate, the questions of *change* and *choice*: what happens now? where do we go from here? and by which means?

To grasp the nature of these questions, and of how they are being answered, one needs to keep in mind the mood – often enough desperate – of Africa in the 1960s. No fewer than two colonial wars are being fought on African soil as I write these words. The first skirmishes in a calamitous racial clash are already taking place in South Africa. Another racial clash, seemingly still avertible, menaces Southern Rhodesia. In the far south, ruled by the dogma of white supremacy, the need for a change of policy is individually vital and internationally momentous. The most ordinary men and women may say and do things which become decisive, not only for themselves but also for their whole community, and beyond it, for the world.

I take the following small but characteristic sample of behaviour from *Fighting Talk*, one of the many South African periodicals that have lately been suppressed. Not long ago this unofficial organ of the Congress resistance movement numbered among its harassed but voluntary distribution agents a young man called Mr E. Musi. His 'area' was among the forests and hills of Pondoland in the east of the Cape Province, one of those places in South Africa with a front of beauty and romance. Neither quality is much present, however, in the story of Mr Musi.

He realized one day that he was wanted by the police. Not, this time, for some usual offence such as carrying the wrong pass or telephoning from the wrong kiosk; but for something more serious. For something, apparently, connected with his efforts at getting *Fighting Talk* into circulation. He was ordered to call at the local forester's office for a parcel of newspapers.

Mr Musi was in trouble. If he did as ordered, he might well

be inviting his own arrest. If he did not, he would be leaving his copies of *Fighting Talk* in the hands of a man who would certainly never let them go any further. How should he behave? He went to the forester's office and collected his parcel.

But his fears were confirmed when he found that the covers were broken.

Just as I thought [he wrote some time later from Basutoland, the British Protectorate to which he had managed to escape]. When I left the office carrying my parcel I nearly crashed with a police van, in which were two policemen, a C.I.D. in uniform and the Public Prosecutor from Mount Ayliff. They had stopped the van at a road-turn near the office, and were standing outside. Just at the time they saw me, they quickly climbed into the van and were driving towards me when I hid the parcel under a block of wood lying near the forest. . . . This is how I left Ndindindi.

The evening I left they were blocking the road near the forest, thinking they would see me coming out of the forest to my room in the workers' quarters. I left them as they were. The following morning they checked at bus stops between Kokstad and Mount Ayliff. I were watching their vans from the mountains. . . .[1]

History does not tell what happened after that, though Mr Musi thought that he would soon be able to slip out from where he was and rescue the papers from under their block of wood. Very largely, Mr Musi's story is South Africa's now. The battle is joined.

Elsewhere, of course, the atmosphere is anything but one of fear and violence. Yet even where it is most peaceful, it is filled with furious argument, not only in the cities and capitals where politicians and intellectuals can be found but also, and perhaps even more, in the little towns and dusty villages where most Africans reside. Anyone who travels much in Africa can bear this out, provided, of course, that the travel is among Africans.

One day in November 1962 I drove some miles off an inland road in order to visit an Iron Age site on the distant slopes of Ngorongoro in northern Tanganyika. Masai elders were settling cases in the shade of a tall tree, much as they must have settled them for untold decades of the past; but not far away, prodding a veil of noonday heat, the familiar flag of TANU, sign and symbol of the Tanganyika African National Union, hung above an office of mud and thatch. A case of mere decoration? Not at all: this village office of TANU was manned. If its staff were not exactly rushed off their feet, they were certainly there.

Pushing on to Mbulu a couple of days later, I found the area commissioner, Mr Shamshama, deep in conference with village delegates of TANU: so deep, indeed, that they kept him up until the small hours of the night because they held, as he explained to me over breakfast next day, that a wrong appointment had been made of a man who 'did not understand his way', who 'could not be trusted as responsible'. The man was an official appointee, and so Mr Shamshama, in his character of government representative in Mbulu Area, loyally defended him. The compromise reached was not without interest. The government saved face by getting the man reappointed as chairman of the committee in question; but the village delegates carried their point by immediately voting him off it again.

'And that stands – what they've done?'

'That stands,' replied Mr Shamshama, nodding a thoughtful head.

But what is true of villagers in Tanganyika is also true of villagers elsewhere. A large debate on the present and the future, on the ways and means of reaching a different kind of life, goes on all over this continent today, and among all sorts and conditions of people.

I mention this mainly to guard against a possible misapprehension from what follows. This book is an attempt to explain and discuss some leading African ideas on political and economic development. In these chapters, inevitably, we shall be largely considering the opinions and decisions of more or less prominent persons: politicians and writers and others who are much in the public eye. But it would be a serious misunderstanding of the real situation to imagine these leaders and would-be leaders as debating merely with each other, before an audience whose minds are so many simple tablets ready for the first emphatic imprint. The leaders of Africa today are in the same basic position as leaders in other countries: their actions and decisions reflect or react to particular scenes and situations, but the common element, in Africa as elsewhere, is the fact of public opinion.

The familiar belief that there is no such thing in Africa as public opinion – *African* public opinion – is another myth of the period now drawing to a close. Whether or not there was such a thing in the distant past – and historical evidence would show that there was – nobody need doubt that African public opinion, in the full meaning of the term, exists today. This view may not be accepted by such rulers as the Portuguese, who explain all nationalist manifestations in their territories as the work of 'communist agitators from outside'; but the evasions of the Portuguese rulers, we may think, do not merit serious attention. Those Europeans in the Rhodesias and Nyasaland who argued, eleven and twelve years ago, that African opposition to British plans for Central African Federation came merely from a 'few subversives', and that 'ninety per cent of the Africans know nothing about it at all',[2] have good reason now to understand how wrong they were.

In what follows we shall review a mass of slogans, solutions, arguments, debates, decisions, and types of political behaviour. Behind them all it will be well to keep in mind the unseen audience, the village audience weighing and deciding for itself, often moved this way or that by audacious oratory or skilful manoeuvre, but still preserving, if sometimes awkwardly and sometimes curiously, a firm and final notion of what is good for ordinary folk and what is not. Even when most apparently abused by the failings of newly independent government, these are the people who will count for most in defining the limits of the possible. It could even be argued that they will count for more than they have usually counted for elsewhere, if only because their ties with leaders and representatives have remained, precisely, close and ever-present.

Such, then, is the company involved: a vast and vividly diverse audience split into a million meetings. Their matter for argument and counter-argument is practically as wide as life itself. Their debate is organized from one end of the continent to the other, whether by vast organizations such as the Union des Populations Camerounaises, with its 3,000 *comités de village*, or by tiny ones like the 'old boys' of the Frafra Youngsters' Union and the Mouvement Autonome de Casamance, or in trade unions which have sometimes formed – as in

Northern Rhodesia and Kenya – a crucial means of political pressure.[3]

Many are still outside the debate. But those who have remained outside, in surviving isolation, are many fewer than ten years ago, fewer still than five years ago, fewer again than one year ago. For this has become a continent in the full ferment of deciding, of trying to decide, of believing that it *can* decide and thinking that it *must* decide, its course into the different years ahead.

It is not difficult to see why this should be so.

Within little more than a decade, two-thirds of Africa has emerged from more or less complete subjection to foreigners – less complete with the British and the French, more with the Belgians – and set out again upon its own.

Viewed across the skylines of history, the colonial period has been little more than an episode, even a brief one; but the skylines of history are distant, and to Africans these fifty or sixty years of foreign domination have been tremendous and traumatic. As we shall see, the impact of these years was always massive, and often terribly destructive. It left Africa with everything to build or rebuild. Many fragments of the 'old society' remained. But all too clearly they could never be put together again. Few people thought they should be. What was needed was a new society, a modern Africa equipped to join the modern world.

Before their political withdrawal some colonial powers, notably the British and the French in their different ways, tried to take a hand in this shaping of a new Africa. They promoted *élites* or 'middle classes', explicitly hoping that their ex-colonisé would model themselves on French or British types of political and economic life; and in due course we shall take a look at the outcome of these efforts. What we must note here is that all these colonies, on becoming independent, were at once faced (whether or not they clearly recognized the fact) by difficult and fundamental problems of post-colonial reorganization.

This is the factor of choice. The liberated cannot go on in the old way, for their old masters have departed. They have to find a new way. This new way may be largely a shadowing of their one-time rulers; or it may be largely an exploration of fresh terrain. Or it may be one of many intermediate solutions, ranging from the mere letting-things-slide, at one extreme, to the other extreme of trying to change everything overnight. Africa can now offer examples of both extremes, as well as of many variants in between.

Faced with this great and urgent reorganization, African politicians and thinkers have embarked on the task of defining what people should want and how they should get it. In doing this they have been led, repeatedly, into reviewing the solutions which other peoples have found or sought. They have had to discover, in so far as that is possible (and it is not so easy as it may sound), what the capitalist countries really mean by free enterprise and what the communist countries really mean by socialism — as well, of course, as investigating the credentials of a large and clamant family of other concepts and ideas. More than this, though — and here again we touch on a central theme in the African awakening — they have been led into thinking back to pre-colonial modes of thought and action; into considering what may be worth trying to conserve or recover from their own traditions of government and ideology; and, increasingly, into attempting a compromise between these major strands of thought and social organization, African and non-African.

In the space of this book I can hope to show only where the main lines of argument and action lead and spread, and to analyse a few probably decisive situations and examples. At this stage of the debate, however, a summary view may perhaps prove more useful than a comprehensive one, at least in promoting the kind of thought and fertile controversy which leads to resolution. We shall certainly miss some interesting details — for which I enter an early apology — yet discussions about African problems have suffered a great deal in the past, or so it seems to me, from minute inspection of the details at the expense of achieving any real idea of the underlying pattern.

New ideas act and react with old ideas. Out of this confused but necessary process a different structure of life will increasingly take shape.

First of all then, if briefly, what were the old ideas?

2 The African Groundwork

The peoples beyond the Sahara, an Italian traveller was reporting in the year 1447 from the oasis of Tuat, 'breed greatly, for a woman bears up to five at a birth'. Since then a great deal more nonsense has been written and believed about Africans. No doubt it could never have been otherwise. To the mariners and merchants of Europe, discoverers by land and sea, these 'natives' appeared as strange and unpredictable as they themselves undoubtedly seemed to the peoples whom they encountered. What is surprising is that much good sense none the less found its way into print. Along with the superstitious and, later, pseudo-scientific rubbish that was fed for centuries to European (and in due course North American) readers, the records reveal a deep vein of 'objective reporting'.

This was true even at the height of the oversea slave trade. Devaluation of African humanity then sank to a depth unequalled in history until South Africa's present rulers came to power. In defence of their practice of wrenching captives out of Africa, a group of Liverpool merchants declared in 1792: 'Africans being the most lascivious of human beings, may it not be imagined that the cries they let forth, at being torn from their wives, proceed from the dread that they will never have the opportunity of indulging their passions in the country to which they are embarking?'

Such attitudes allowed no respect either for the victims or for the peoples from whom they came. To those who condemned the trade, British governments of the day replied that it was far too profitable to be stopped. 'We cannot,' said Lord Dartmouth, Secretary of State for the Colonies in 1775, 'allow the Colonies to check or to discourage in any degree a traffic so beneficial to the nation.' The argument was persuasive: just how much so we are well placed to understand in the 1960s. Nearly two centuries after Lord Dartmouth had enunciated his views on the indispensable benefits of the slave trade, another British government returned almost word for word the same reply to critics who condemned the sale of arms to the Republic of South Africa. The sale might have its unfortunate side; it was far too profitable to be stopped.

Yet even during the darkest years of the slave trade there were Englishmen and other Europeans in Africa who had begun to adopt a new attitude to the 'natives'. Their writings – one thinks, for example, of Dr Thomas Winterbottom, physician to the colony of Sierra Leone at the end of the eighteenth century – struck a new note of factual and even scientific inquiry. These investigators formed the slender pioneering column of all those later men and women who have laboured in the field of understanding Africa. And if today it remains true that a great deal of nonsense is still being written about Africans, it is also true that many of the sillier myths are being swept away. The verdict of modern scholarship is that the past of Africa is both long and interesting and contains the record of a continuous and in some significant ways highly successful development over several thousand years. This development gives no ground for any assumption of natural inferiority or even – quite surprisingly often – of any comparative failure in achievement.

Much of that development belongs to an Iron Age which is known to have begun about two thousand years ago, and to have involved, in the words of two British historians, 'a considerable fund of common political ideas'.[4]

What were these political ideas?

This is not the place to inquire deeply into the growth of pre-colonial cultures and civilizations in Africa. The point to notice here is that Africa's political and social history is neither new nor simple. On the contrary, a wide range of its underlying ideology undoubtedly goes back into a remote past.

Any comprehensive history of Africa that may be written in the future – and it cannot be written yet – will have to set Ancient Egypt, for example, near the centre of its picture, both because Egypt was a transmitter of ideas from Asia and, probably more important in the long run, because Egypt was the exploiter and developer of social and economic trends already indigenous to Africa. Moreover, as an outstanding French Egyptologist has lately observed, 'perhaps the greatest service Egyptology can offer is to furnish, as no other branch of study can, precious chronological points of departure for the ancient history of Africa'.[5]

But all this would provide only the beginning to the story of Africa's political development. Partly growing out of it, partly evolving new forms by reaction with pressures inside Africa and with other pressures from outside Africa, later history has produced a multiplicity of political and social patterns (and, of course, economic, religious, and artistic patterns as well): a multiplicity, indeed, as great as the varied and challenging nature of African experience and environment.

Anthropologists and historians have grappled with the task of sorting out these patterns into a manageably small number of leading types and categories. Not surprisingly, they have trouble with their terms. What, for instance, is a tribe? My *Pocket Oxford Dictionary* (but the longer versions merely elaborate) explains that a tribe is a 'group of people in a primitive or barbarous stage of development acknowledging the authority of a chief and usually regarding themselves as having a common ancestor'. This is well enough as far as it goes; but it does not go very far. The Yoruba of Western Nigeria are often called a tribe, at least by Europeans. Certainly they acknowledge the authority of their chiefs and generally regard themselves as having common ancestors: can we really believe that they are therefore 'primitive and barbarous'? Nobody who knows them will say so.

Of course it is true that the word 'tribe' has generally been used as a term of abuse. This is now unfashionable. 'Anyone who wants to use it [tribe] as a technical term, and not a term of abuse,' warns Dr Lucy Mair, 'should be clear that it simply means an independent political division of a population with a common culture.'[6] Like the Lowland Scots, perhaps, in the United Kingdom?

Mair, of course, was thinking of Africa, and specifically of

East Africa. But Huntingford, thinking of the same region, goes further. A tribe in East Africa, he argues, 'is a group united by a common name in which the members take a pride, by a common language, by a common territory, and by a feeling that all who do not share this name are outsiders, "enemies" in fact'.[7] If this is true, as it appears to be, then why is a 'tribe' any different from a 'nation'? Isn't it mere mystification to describe a typical European people, with all their xenophobia, group-ambition, and sense of exclusivist pride, as a *nation*, while reserving the word *tribe* ('primitive and barbarous' being understood) for a people like the Yoruba? Such mystification, one cannot help feeling, is in no small part the fault of anthropologists who have generally cultivated a habit, when writing about African societies, of creeping in at the back door of political reality instead of marching boldly up the front steps.

The matter of names is not without importance, for it connects with the larger question of what actually happened. The usual picture of pre-colonial Africa – except for the Muslim states of the north, though even these were generally reduced in reputation to 'nests of piratical fanatics' – was presented in our standard works, at least until a few years ago, as one of unrelieved and hopeless chaos or stagnation. Such primitive segments of the human race, it was understandably concluded, could not possibly have possessed a *political* history of their own. Or none, at any rate, that was worth talking about.

No serious historian has any such conviction nowadays. The last ten or twenty years have completely revised the standard view of African society, whether past or present, and with this revision there has come a need for a new terminology. So far, it must be said, new terms to describe the specific social and political systems of Africa are largely lacking, and we are obliged, for want of better, to make do with what we have from other lands.

Some familiar terms are clearly fitting. It is now agreed that a very large number of African peoples moved out of truly primitive forms of organization (during an Iron Age which began some two thousand years ago) into forms that can be called *states* and *empires*. Some of these remained at a simple stage of inner complexity; others moved into far from simple patterns of bureaucratic authority. Many based their means of government – and their central revenues – on types of loyalty and tribute which resemble feudalism. Quite a few British scholars reject this particular term, though on grounds which appear at the very least controversial; meanwhile they seem to find it difficult to suggest anything better, and accordingly take refuge in circumambient explanations which tend to finish where they begin.[8]

But whatever one may think of the credentials of African feudalism, there remains the fact, agreed by all whose opinions are of weight, that many African peoples formed themselves into states; and that some of these states grew into recognizably imperial solutions of the central 'question of power' – the question, that is to say, of *who* are to be the rulers and *whom* they are to rule. This process of 'state-forming', moreover, began a long time ago. It began most clearly of all in those regions where easy movement by man and horse made military and political enclosure possible and worthwhile: in North Africa, in the wide grasslands of the Sudan, and, not long after that (though seldom with the horse), in the forest fringe of Guinea and, later again (but never with the horse), in the vast woods and prairies of the centre and the south.

Two well-known medieval sources indicate what outsiders may have thought of such developments in Africa. An Arab of the Hejaz travelled down the East African coast somewhat more than a thousand years ago, gathered information from sailors and merchants, and afterwards wrote a memorable book which he entitled, not without a conscious touch of romance, *The Meadows of Gold and Mines of Gems*. He described a large African state near the mouths of the Zambezi River. This state was governed by a king whose authority rested on election, for he was chosen 'to govern the people with equity', and reached over the heads of many lesser kings in the neighbour-hood. Al Masʿudi explained in his book that this 'king of kings' could none the less be deposed if he abused his power of government or failed to use it wisely. Altogether Al Masʿudi appears to be describing a very typical chieftainship or kingship among a wide range of African peoples. There might well have been applied to this south-east African monarch of a thousand years ago the same traditional standards as those which Rattray recorded for the chiefs of Ashanti in 1929. These were 'enstooled' to the tune of the following public admonitions:

> Tell him that
> We do not wish for greediness
> We do not wish that he should curse us
> We do not wish that his ears should be hard of hearing
> We do not wish that he should call people fools
> We do not wish that he should act on his own initiative
> We do not wish things done as in Kumasi
> We do not wish that it should ever be said
>   'I have no time. I have no time.'
> We do not wish personal abuse
> We do not wish personal violence.[9]

West Africa, or at least the Western Sudan, was nearer to the Muslim states of the Mediterranean, and their scholars were better informed about it than they were about remote East Africa. In 1067, just a year after William of Normandy had won the Battle of Hastings, an Andalusian Arab named al Bekri published an account of political organization in the Western Sudan. Drawing on much evidence from travellers and soldiers who had been there (Morocco had lately invaded the Western Sudan in force), al Bekri showed that a considerable segment of the West African grasslands had long lain within the power of a single state, and that this empire could be reckoned as a notable enemy or ally.

'Ghana is the title of the kings of that people,' he wrote, 'and the name of their country is Aoukar. Their present king is called Tenkamenin. He came to the throne in [1062] . . . and is the master of a large empire and of a formidable power. . . .' Having described Tenkamenin's court and courtiers, al Bekri went on to illustrate the nature of his political organization. Using this account with other Arab sources, one may see that Ghana's power rested partly on a strong central organization which could raise military levies of a feudal type, and partly on an intelligent exploitation of the gold and salt trade.

Salt was vital to the people of these torrid grasslands, as it still is; but in those days the best deposits of salt lay northward on the fringe of the Sahara. From there, too, Western Sudanese peoples had their copper. But gold came from the south, from the fringe of the forest belt or the forest belt itself. What the lords of Ghana essentially achieved – and in this they were followed by other imperial rulers later on – was to win political control over the means of sending out gold to the north and, at the same time, over the means of bringing in salt to the south. Thus they could and did draw revenues both from the import of salt and copper and the goods of North Africa, and from the export of gold and ivory. 'The king,' notes al Bekri in a key passage, 'imposes a tax of a dinar of gold on every donkey-load of salt that enters his country, and of two dinars on every load that leaves. A load of copper pays him five *mitcals*' (perhaps five-eighths of an ounce of gold, though the *mitcal* varied wildly in weight), 'and a load of miscellaneous goods pays him ten.'

Not only that. The king also saw to it that he monopolized the trade in gold, at least near its source. 'All pieces of gold found in the mines of the empire' – the gold will have come, in fact, mainly from alluvial deposits – 'belong to the king, but he lets the public have the dust which is everywhere familiar. Without this restriction, gold would become so abundant as practically to lose its value.' The kings of Ghana well understood their business. West African gold lay at the root of their revenues. It would remain so for their successors. Three hundred years after al Bekri an English king began importing West African gold for the new currency he meant to strike. And 'guinea' is still a word we use.

Thus in their *capacity* to raise revenues, responding to their *need* to finance the workings of an empire, the rulers of Ghana had clearly reached a stable pattern of political sophistication. They were not, of course, modern dictators: behind the bare record of their doings one must imagine a kind of feudal authority resting on governors and chiefs and military henchmen, sub-chiefs and tributary peoples, all of these being enmeshed in their turn in a more or less coherent order of society. This system, together with its notable successor states and empires, occupies a complex and important place in the West African record. All this, by the same token, is part of the groundwork of Africa today.

Political history may be variously defined. My own definition would agree with those who hold that political history consists in analysing and illustrating how social authority was organized, distributed, and applied at any given place and time: of seeing how, in short, the central 'question of power' was actually settled by a given people or peoples.

But if this is a reasonable statement of what we are about, clearly we cannot rest content with looking only at societies and structures which achieved kingship. The fact is that many peoples reacted to the problems of their development and environment by evolving simple or embryonic forms of government, and that these systems served them well enough to endure for centuries. These primitive systems of government – primitive in the sense that they made do with rudimentary means of organizing, distributing, and applying social authority – are also part of the record. They cannot be ignored without serious distortion.

It may be said, broadly, that the origins of political history in this continent belong to the beginnings of the Iron Age, to the period of early struggle with an often hostile physical environment. New techniques of migration and cultivation, based on the iron spear and probably on the iron hoe, married with new methods of social organization and led on to the growth, wherever circumstances proved favourable, of large political systems such as Ghana. Here and there, however, the centralizing process whereby peoples came together within the tightening zone of a king's authority was partly lacking or was largely muted. Often enough, it remained altogether absent.

Of the latter cases, some of the most interesting (or, at any rate, the best studied) have occurred in the waterlogged lands of the Upper Nile, not far from the northern borders of Uganda, where such peoples as the Nuer and the Dinka have their home. Other cases may of course be found elsewhere: in parts of East Africa and West Africa, and, though on a different level of social growth, among the Pygmies and Bushmen of central and southern Africa.

These peoples have governed themselves in a great variety of ways. But most of them have been alike in living without any form of strong central rule, without states (much less empires), and often without any obvious or formal means of maintaining law and order and of prosecuting war and trade. It has been none the less abundantly shown that such people have generally possessed a workable and durable system for ensuring individual and even collective security, although their systems have seldom comprised any of the recognizable hierarchies of political power that make and enforce social rules and judgements. 'Among the Nuer,' according to Mair, 'no individual anywhere has authority to say whether fighting is permissible or to command that it should cease.'[10] This does not mean that the Nuer are satisfied with 'savage anarchy'. On the contrary, they have worked out and learned how to apply a great many useful rules about the conduct and control of society, though they have done so by means of an absolute minimum of delegated authority.

This apparent 'simplicity of tribal life' has misled many observers into supposing that people like the Nuer have lived with 'no rules at all'. It is now seen, by contrast, that Nuer government (if we may use the word for an authority so little and loosely formulated) is in fact a distinctive *system* of society, and that this system is the product of a long and difficult self-adjustment to a highly specialized land and climate. Technically at a primitive level of life, the Nuer are organizationally at a point that is anything but primitive.

For how do you live and survive if your land is under water half the year? What do you do if your environment contains neither metals nor stone, or none that you can get at? Where do you look for help if your neighbours live in the same way, or, far across the skyline, offer you no friendly hand? Lost in their enormous swamps and sodden grasslands, dwelling in scattered homesteads, the Nuer and their neighbours have not been discouraged. They have found a point of balance between the waters and the scorching sun on one hand, and the demands of cattle and a little cultivation on the other. The trouble with the Nuer, if it is a trouble, is that they have succeeded so well in attaining a stability which calls within itself for no change at all.

Contemplating their regular and so gently poised adjustment, one may better understand why many so-called primitive tribes have contented themselves with their own culture.

Obedience to an accepted pattern of behaviour, the sanctioned product of long trial and error, was the condition of life itself: deviation could only bring disaster. This seemed and often was so true that men and women could implicitly believe it, and could see in social change nothing but foolishness or danger. Here, of course, one may comprehend why 'tribal life' required and applied such strict and all-embracing patterns of moral sanction on the behaviour of the individual. The stagnation of the Nuer, if that is what it is, precisely illustrates the *political* success of their development.

It is easy to exaggerate the apparent stagnation of 'tribal Africa'. These societies were the outcome of much and varied adjustment to a difficult environment. Emerging from a remote past, they went on growing or shifting in power and efficiency, changing their habits, meeting new challenges, evolving new patterns. Those that were successful – those that have survived – have revealed a marked capacity for adapting to new situations and for adopting new ideas. Much of the story of the African Iron Age is one of perpetual movement across the vast land mass of inner Africa by peoples who went through zone after zone of contrasting climate, soil, vegetation, and therefore means of livelihood. Stability and change play an underlying counterpoint in the African song.

Peopling their continent, the Africans brought in cereals and began cultivating them, learned how to raise cattle, adapted metal tools and weapons to their own use, undertook mining and smelting and forging on a continental scale, borrowed crops from other lands, introduced soil conservation and terrace agriculture where hillsides needed these, discovered the medicinal value of a host of herbs and plants, and worked out their own explanations of mankind and the universe. All this had taken place long before the first ships set forth from Europe.

But then and afterwards the slow and often painful processes of change continued. With new challenges – in the form of muskets, to take one important example – some of the older systems of 'minimal government' could not suffice. They had to be modified, made over into other systems nearer to or identical with those we recognize as states and empires. This occurred at all levels of political organization. At one end of the spectrum there were changes of imperial structure in the Western Sudan or the plateau lands of what is now Rhodesia; at the other, at the extreme of 'minimal government', new conditions encouraged simple village headmen to become 'kings and nobles', the better to wield their power but also, no doubt, the better to defend their people.

The examples are legion. One may trace the force of political change in every corner of the continent, and among peoples large or small. Thus the little Anuak clans of the west Ethiopian borderlands, obtaining muskets from their neighbours, developed an aristocracy. The chiefless peoples of the Tanganyika plains, facing a time of troubles, acquired chiefs. The numerous and enterprising clans of the Ashanti, persecuted by their neighbours, came together in a union made indissoluble by a ritual object – the famous Golden Stool – invented for the purpose. Menaced by the slave trade, the scattered peoples of the Niger delta founded city-states and engaged in that curious trade themselves. Harried by Zulu regiments, the clans of the Drakensberg foothills formed themselves into the Basuto nation. And it was the same with the arts of peace. New technologies passed from people to people. Social norms expanded or contracted according to the pressure of the times.

All this, really, is just a way of saying that Africa's huge diversity of experience and environment has found a full reflection in the political and economic structures of daily life. Here in this capacious continental home there has been room for many contrasting phases of social growth to exist at one and the same time. There has been tolerance for many exceptions to the broadest rule of group behaviour. A few Stone Age peoples still live alongside neighbours who entered the Iron Age fifteen or twenty centuries back. Chiefless peoples still border on others who have kings and 'kings of kings'. 'Minimal government' still goes on side by side with 'maximal government'.

Nothing in all this, surely, can leave room for thinking that peoples who have stayed content with primitive forms of government are therefore of lesser talent or intelligence than their hierarchical neighbours. I emphasize this point because there has sometimes been a tendency to suppose that this or that people, according to the sheer complexity of its political and social system, is really 'superior' to folk who have never seen the point of having chiefs and policemen. To think like this would be to adopt, in Anene's words, 'an out-of-date assumption that a moral hierarchy exists as regards centralized political organizations and what are usually described as segmented societies'.[11]

If historians of Africa have tended to emphasize the states-and-empires side of the story, this is largely because they have had to meet the bland assumption of European culture that no such states and empires ever existed, that Africans have therefore had no history worth the name and so no historical identity – and therefore, reaching at last the bottom of this line of thought, no claim to an inherent equality with Europeans. But the true study of history has reference only to experience and environment. Had all the peoples in the world developed in the same environment and under the same conditions of experience, no doubt they would all have developed in the same way: as it is, they have developed in a myriad different ways in response to as many different circumstances, and this is what history is about.

The diversity of African politics in the past, however, is only half the picture. The other half is not much less important. It consists of an underlying unity. Most of the populations of sub-Saharan Africa (and it may well have been true of North Africa before the Arab invasions of the eighth century) have shared close relationships to a single body of cultural beliefs and modes of behaviour. This is the reason why a purely regional study of the African past can never hope to yield the true keys to an understanding of Africa, nor reveal the richness of experience that lies within a pattern and social process continental in their scope.

In point of language, for example – the figure of 800 languages, according to Fortune, is a conservative one[12] – it now appears that the diversity is based on a unity provided by three basic groups. That in itself might seem to be saying little enough, but the statement wears a different aspect when one considers that the largest of these three groups is evidently parent to 'nearly all the languages of west and central Africa, east and south Africa'.[13] That again might seem to exclude large segments of the continent from the common cultural foundations to which I have alluded. Yet this, too, wears a different garb as soon as one remembers that many of the forms of kingship and religion that grew powerful in central and southern Africa were forms known and used by peoples of the far north, whether in the Nile Valley or along the fertile grasslands of the Saharan fringe. The familiar division of Africa into 'south and north of the Sahara' may be wonderfully convenient, but it can also be misleading. If the Sahara was undoubtedly a daunting obstacle to movement back and forth across its plains, it was seldom or never a true dividing line.

It seems clear that a number of common factors have profoundly influenced and worked on the majority of populations in the continent. Their basic ethnic and linguistic unities, now becoming ever more apparent, have had the firm cement of cultural unities as well. These have been economic, political, and ideological. Without attempting to develop this line of thought in any detail, I should like to suggest where it runs and leads.

The root problem, as we have seen, was to survive and if possible prosper in circumstances that were often very hostile. To an initially poor range of foodstuffs, there were added the yam and the banana some two thousand years ago (probably from south-east Asia) and much later, with the coming of the Portuguese, a number of valuable crops from South America. This economy could seldom or never be intensive outside the Nile Valley and a few other favoured spots. But it seems to have been stable. It seems to have produced a regular overspill of population from the north-central areas into the centre and the south. Whenever this happened, families or clans or groups of clans moved in search of fresh land. And so the whole central and southern region of the continent, a vast and varied region of forest and marsh and grassland, was gradually peopled by folk of the same ethnic and linguistic stock. These populations split into a multitude of recognizably different peoples; and in this way there arose, across the gap and gulf of time, the many hundred variants of the Bantu language family.

This process, greatly simplified in this short explanation, likewise produced what Dr Audrey Richards has called 'the common features of Bantu political organization'.[14] These features – and they are not in fact limited to the Bantu language group – may be subsumed as: a family unit that is 'extended', encompassing many degrees of relationship besides those of husband–wife and parents–children; a strong emphasis of descent through family group and clan group; an almost universal tendency to make political authority dependent on family and lineage; and a loyalty to chieftainship that is linked to spiritual as well as temporal power.

And this in turn explains another set of common features: those that emphasize a basic unity of social behaviour and religious belief. Much of traditional African law illustrates the point. 'I conceive that land,' a Nigerian chief told the West African Lands Committee in 1912, 'belongs to a vast family of which many are dead, few are living, and countless members are unborn'. This idea is familiar in many regions of Africa. 'The universality of this concept throughout both Sudanese and Bantu Africa,' Elias writes, 'has been confirmed again and again wherever indigenous societies have been studied.'[15] Only last year a group of Ugandan students in London began publishing a discussion journal dedicated to 'the dead, the living, and the unborn'.[16]

Far from 'bowing down to wood and stone', as the old cliché had it, Africans are now understood to have long possessed religions and metaphysical systems – many of them (perhaps most) more or less clearly related to one another – worthy of serious attention. Man and the world were created at the behest of a Supreme God by the agency of lesser gods, and all these and other spiritual powers are worshipped or respected or implored by sacrifice and prayer. Beneath the gods are lesser powers, often evil, sometimes benign, occasionally both, who may be conjured by magical procedures much in the manner of traditional Europe – much in the manner, no doubt, of all pre-scientific societies. Long regarded by Europeans as squalid if not altogether contemptible, many African religions are now understood to have been – indeed, often still to be – as valid and respectable, within the terms of a non-materialist explanation of life and death, as any other in the world. Even the ghastly witch-doctor, so long a figure of gruesome terror to the European eye, turns out on closer acquaintance to be little different in his intentions from the family doctor round the corner.

All these 'factors of underlying unity', as they may reasonably be called, have their bearing on the political growth of modern Africa. They are as vital to the 'native background' as the diversity they support, or as the 'foreign contribution' we shall now consider.

3 The Foreign Contribution

A giraffe arriving at the Chinese court in 1415, together with ambassadors from the East African city-state of 'Ma-lin', was understandably received with some attention. The emperor himself agreed to welcome it with stately ceremonial. Accompanied by a 'celestial horse', which was probably a zebra, and a 'celestial stag', which was possibly an oryx, this unlikely beast from the uttermost ends of the western sea was felt to be a singular though not surprising token of worldwide respect. Besides, its safe arrival was something of a triumph. Its arduous journey had taken it across the Indian Ocean to Ceylon or southern India and thence, by trans-shipment, onward to China.

This giraffe in any case deserves a place in history, for the ceremonial obligation to accompany ambassadors from distant countries home was among the reasons why the renowned Admiral Ch'eng-lo sailed for 'Ma-lin' in 1417, and thus made China's first attested landfall on Africa. Chinese–African trade had previously gone through many intermediaries; now for a few brief years there was direct if rare intercourse. I mention the fact as a comment on the frequent assertion that continental Africa possessed no knowledge of the outside world until the arrival of Europeans. The element of isolation was undoubtedly a real one, especially in central and southern Africa; but the isolation was never complete.

East Africa and the Eastern world were long involved in a two-way traffic of much value to both, as also were West Africa and the Muslim North from Morocco to Egypt. The more we learn of the past, the more clearly we may recognize that these inter-penetrating influences were many and important. Of those that came from outside, Islam was among the greatest. It won the loyalty of a number of West African leaders and some of their peoples at least from the eleventh century A.D.: fine tombstones of Spanish marble more than 900 years old, found near Gao on the Middle Niger and carrying Muslim inscriptions in Arabic, bear witness to this. Other disciples of Muhammad converted the little towns and trading settlements of coastal East Africa; in time the peoples of these places built a notable Muslim civilization of their own. Operating radically in the political field, Islam helped to break down tribal barriers and form new states.

All such influences and ideas and techniques from outside Africa, entering the continent over many centuries through its peripheral borderlands in east and north, were additions to the stock of African thought and behaviour. These additions could be absorbed and used, and often were, without destroying the general fabric of traditional society. They modified the fabric, introduced new strands and colours and patterns, provoked new forms and fashions; yet the overall effect was almost always one of reinforcement and renewal, not of destruction. The European colonial impact, however, was not like this. Its impact, generally, was altogether different both in kind and in degree. Nothing like it had been seen or known before; and nothing afterwards could ever be at all the same again. The reasons are various. They lay partly in the sheer destructiveness of the methods employed. Yet there was something in this conquest that was even more ruinous of existing society than forced labour, firearms, and the rest could ever be by themselves. This new factor was the expansive nature of European civilization.

It can be shown without much difficulty that the leading states of Africa and Europe were divided in medieval times, five or six hundred years ago, by no 'cultural gap' of any great significance. Law and order in the Western Sudan were probably superior under the earlier emperors of Mali than in contemporary France and England, while the scholarship of Timbuktu and Djenne could possibly have given points to that of Oxford or Paris. But the 'cultural gap' between Africa and Europe at the beginning of the colonial period, a hundred years ago, was so wide that many Europeans found it genuinely difficult to believe that Africans were altogether human. No doubt the gap in 1860 was really less enormous than it seemed to European travellers of the time, few of whom were men of learning or reflection. All the same, it was a gap which spanned, for Europe, the displacement of superstition by science, of handicraft manufacture by industrialism, of feudal politics by modern politics, and of primitive trading by the skills of a highly ingenious capitalism.

Thus the Europe which invaded Africa was an entirely different Europe from medieval times, while Africa, if by no means unchanged within itself, was still in the age before science and industrialism. To ask why Europe should have advanced so far ahead of others would open an unending detour: the Chinese, one may note in passing, had led the world in technological achievement until the fifteenth century only to come to a long halt for reasons which scholars still discuss without agreement. The point to remember here is that this differential between an invading Europe and an invaded Africa proved crushing to traditional society.

This is where the 'foreign contribution' becomes for the first time absolutely decisive. Yet if the colonial period was in a large sense revolutionary, its revolution was a strange one. Its contribution was not to build or even lay foundations for the new society that Africa needed; what it did was to open the way for the new by undermining the old. Contrary to the claims of its prophets, colonial rule did not 'civilize' Africa, or modernize Africa in any meaningful sense of the word, much less leave Africans with the mere job of taking over the prepared positions of a new social structure. Philanthropic individuals and institutions may have worked hard for the good of Africans; their saving labours, though often brave and even generous, could never be more than palliative and peripheral. For while colonial rule built a few roads and railways and opened a few mines and plantations (though for its own convenience and enrichment), dropping here and there a few crumbs of educational and social enlightenment, its central effect was one of dismantlement. Within its new frontiers, it took apart; it did not put together again.

But this central effect of dismantlement, though generally negative, has been none the less decisive. In the wake of colonial rule, an independent Africa can no longer continue in anything resembling its pre-colonial condition. It will now either suffer a new subjection or it will 'catch up' and live fully in the modern

35

world. It will either start to build a new society, or it will collapse into chaos.

We can divide Africa's experience of Europe into five main phases.

First there was mutual discovery. In this the Portuguese of the fifteenth century were the true pioneers, leading the rest of sea-going Europe down the long west coast and far beyond. These early encounters were few and far between. They were accompanied by much raiding and piracy from European ships, but gradually settled to an often peaceful trading partnership.

This partnership in commerce lasted in one way or another for nearly four centuries. Concerned at first with African gold and ivory and peppers, and with European cottons and metalware, the trade soon deviated into a wholesale transport of African captives for enslavement in Europe's new mines and plantations of Brazil, the Caribbean, Central and North America.

For Africa, this traffic in humanity was disastrous. But for Europe it became a considerable source of wealth. During this second phase of contact with Africa (and partly thanks to it), England and France began their industrial revolution. Europeans also started to explore inner Africa. Apart from a few lone wanderers, like Park in the Western Sudan and Bruce in Ethiopia and along the Upper Nile, discovery was concentrated for West and South Africa in the decades of about 1820 to 1860, and somewhat later for the eastern and central regions. There was still no conquest but for a few forays by the Portuguese, whether in Angola and Moçambique or along the middle reaches of the Zambezi, and the slow spread of Boer and afterwards British penetration from the Cape of Good Hope.

A third phase of closer European involvement, arising from the ending of the second, came with the abolition of the oversea slave trade, the growth of European imperialism and its internecine rivalries, the use of quinine against malaria, and, on the whole, a new capacity (whether military, economic, or political) for effective conquest. All these and other factors began to mature soon after the middle of the nineteenth century. They set the scene for colonial invasion and partition, which began, with a fourth phase, some seventy or eighty years ago.

Today another phase opens with the rise of African independence and a relationship, at last, of mutual respect. But here and now we are concerned with the years between about 1880 (though colonial rule had in fact already begun at a few points along the coast) and 1960, the year that crowned Africa's modern assumption of responsibility for her own affairs.

All these phases, setting off chains of action and reaction of the most diverse kinds, properly belong to 'the foreign contribution'. They became generally decisive for political and economic change, however, only with the fourth phase: that of conquest, annexation, and partition.

The dismantlement of traditional society occurred in different ways, military, political, social, and economic. Most painful, though perhaps least influential on the course of history, was the purely physical destruction. This varied with time and place and person; not infrequently it was severe. Nobody knows how severe it really was, because vital statistics are missing, as are many of the records. 'They can have my Congo,' King Leopold remarked in 1908, when the Belgian Parliament took over responsibility for the Congo Free State, 'but they've no right to know what I've done there'; and he proceeded to a great bonfire of documents.[17] Yet many documents survived. In 1919 Belgium's official Commission for the Protection of the Natives could estimate that the population of the Congo might have been as much as *halved* since the beginning of European occupation some forty years earlier.

Of course the degree of violence and destruction greatly varied. Often enough there was little or none, and sometimes the colonial conquest was the means of bringing peace to ravaged lands. European accounts have naturally tended to emphasize the pacific side of the process; Africans, reacting the other way, have tended to ignore it. On the whole, the violence would seem to have been more frequent than Europeans have lately cared to remember. Men like Carl Peters, the imperial German agent in East Africa, were certainly exceptional. Replying to overtures for peace from the ruler of the Gogo, Peters replied (and so recorded in his memoirs): 'The Sultan shall have peace. . . . Plunder the village, set fire to the houses, and smash everything to pieces that will not burn!' He was as good as his word, and not only on that occasion. 'Everywhere the spectacle was repeated. After a short resistance the Gogo fled in all directions; burning brands were thrown into the houses, and the axes did their work in hewing the pieces which could not be burnt.'[18] Yet such conduct, though unusual, was by no means unique.

When we come to the French and British, the case grows rather more complex. Initially, their impact was often little less severe than that of the Germans in East or South West Africa. We shall never know how much damage was done to the South African Bantu-speaking peoples by those 'kaffir Wars' that filled so much of the nineteenth century; while the military expeditions of the French from Senegal eastwards were seldom conducted with much respect for 'the rules of war'. In their equatorial territories the French likewise applied the same frantic system of exploitation by concession companies that had made such havoc in Leopold's Congo. Returning in 1905 to the countries he had helped to win for France, the explorer de Brazza observed in bitter disillusionment that 'ruin and terror have been visited on this unhappy colony'.

Yet physical destruction was not the underlying long-range factor in social dislocation. Africa had yielded millions of captives for slave labour in the Americas, but traditional systems of government had largely held firm through all the period of 'human export', or else adjusted themselves to circumstances they could no longer hope to control. Africa's traditional systems might have survived the colonial blood-letting as well, and even the political impact of colonial rule in itself, since colonial rulers (or the less short-sighted among them) were often well enough pleased to compound with willing chiefs and elders. What swept away the means of such survival (even though the appearance of survival might often still persist) was the economic intervention of the invaders.

With this, too, the impact greatly varied. In territories of white settlement there was an immediate drive to enclose vast regions of land within which Africans could no longer farm or live except as labourers. South Africa and Southern Rhodesia have become the outstanding examples, though Kenya and Algeria have run them close. By 1951, for example, the amount of land 'scheduled for African occupation' in South Africa was no more than 9·6 per cent of the whole country; today, with a few additions forced by the sheer pressure of rural overcrowding, it is still less than 12 per cent, the rest being kept for Europeans. When several million peasants are stuffed away like this, the consequences can only be disastrous, both for their land and for themselves. A White Paper of 1936 remarked of the South African 'Native Reserves' that 'speaking generally,' they were 'congested, denuded, overstocked, eroded, and for the most part in a deplorable condition';[19] and yet this was the way in which rural Africa was supposed to survive.

At the other end of Africa, Algeria has offered another spectacle of 'ruin by enclosure'. Here again the real cause of destruction lay not so much in the greed of individuals as in the system they promoted. Before its intensive occupation by the French, the fertile coastwise uplands of Algeria had been profitable producers of food for home consumption, notably cereals and mutton. But French settlers had no interest in growing food for the local market and turned, almost from the first, to the production of wine for export. The area under vines rose from a mere 4,000 acres in 1830 to no fewer than 750,000 acres in 1953.

Algerians began feeling a new hunger. For while the production of cereals had remained at about the same level since the 1880s, the population (thanks largely to modern medicine) had almost tripled in the same period. It has been calculated that the average Algerian had five quintals of grain a year in 1871, four in 1900, but only 2½ in 1940. The situation on the eve of the great insurrection of 1954 was that fewer than one thousand European landowners possessed about one-seventh of all cultivable land outside the barren southern regions, while more than half a million peasant *families* had no land at all.

Yet land was useless without labour, and so were mining concessions. The enclosure of land and the opening of mines went hand-in-hand with pressure on rural Africans to leave their homes and work for European wages, or rather, since wages were altogether inadequate, for European employers. It is here that we arrive at what was probably the most destructive element in the economic system of the invaders.

Directly forced labour was used in all colonies, though seldom

39

in a massive way except in the Congo Free State and the early years of the Belgian Congo, in the French equatorial territories, and in the Portuguese colonies. Of course there are exceptions to this statement (as there are to every generalization about Africa): the Boer farmers of the south were (and still are) accustomed to regard Africans as natural slaves, while the toll of forced labour exacted by European colonial administrators of all nationalities, up and down the continent, defies reasonable estimate. But generally it remains true that the British and the French early came to prefer *indirect* methods of forcing Africans to work for Europeans. Their approach was simple. They applied a money tax to peasants who lived without money. Either the peasants earned the money to pay the tax, which meant going to work for Europeans – or the police seized them for 'punishment', which meant, of course, the same thing. Out of this system, and the evasions and resistances that it evoked, a conviction arose among Europeans that Africans were feckless, idle, and incapable of responsible work.*

It is hard to exaggerate the extent and the effects of this imposition of the need to work for Europeans on countless millions of subsistence-farmers and their dependents. It went on everywhere, and it went on recklessly. Large areas were denuded of their 'fit adult males' for long periods of time. Huge populations adjusted to colonial rule by taking it increasingly for granted that their men would annually leave home and 'migrate' to the towns and mines and white plantations. The resultant impoverishment of rural life – and we shall return to this central point – was often calamitous. Thick volumes of evidence emphasize this fact. Here a couple of examples will have to suffice.

What the effect of migrant labour could be on a previously stable society was indicated by an official report for Nyasaland

---

* King Leopold provides the characteristic comment on forced labour – direct or indirect – as on so many other aspects of early colonial practice. Refusing in 1905 to stop forcing Congolese to collect rubber for him, he said that the coercive system might be changed 'when the Negro has generally shaken off his idleness and become ready to work for the lure of wages alone'. Meanwhile, though Leopold omitted to say so, rubber-collecting remained as cheap for the agents of the Congo Free State as it was costly in health and even life for the Congolese who were forced to do the work. For Leopold's further attitudes, see Professor Jean Stengers's penetrating analysis of relations between the Belgian Parliament and their 'King of the Congo': *Belgique et Congo: L'Elaboration de la Charte Coloniale*, Brussels, 1963.

in 1935, by which time the system had been in operation for many years. 'The whole fabric of the old order of society,' commented this grave though cautious report, 'is undermined when 30 to 60 per cent of the able-bodied men are absent at one time' – as was the case in Nyasaland by then. 'Emigration [on this scale], which destroys the old, offers nothing to take its place, and the family–community is threatened with complete dissolution.'[20]

The gross effect, one may repeat, was serious and continuous dismantlement of the pattern and structure of social life. And this was compensated by no corresponding gain in understanding and advancement by the men who went away to industrial work. For they went to the mines of the Rand or the Rhodesian Copperbelt, and there they worked as unskilled labourers beneath a colour bar of white enforcement. And this bar for long denied them access to any real participation in the new world of industry they were supposed to have entered.

Nyasaland may be regarded as having existed at one extreme of the migrant-labour pressure and experience, for this was a colony of relatively benign and gentle rule. At another extreme there lie the Portuguese colonies. According to the report of a senior Portuguese Inspector of Colonies in 1947, the situation in Angola 'is in some ways worse than simple slavery. Under slavery, after all, the native is bought as an animal: his owner prefers him to remain as fit as a horse or an ox. Yet here [in Angola] the native is not bought – he is hired from the State, although he is called a free man. And his employer cares little if he sickens or dies, once he is working, because when he sickens or dies his employer will simply ask for another.'[21] One could pile on the evidence; abstracted from its emotive context, the effect was once again one of widespread and continuous undermining of traditional life and welfare.

The colonial period may itself be divided into a number of sub-periods. *Invasion* was one of these. *Pacification,* as it was called, was another: a protracted period, this one, to the point that Belgian Congo archives, for example, can reveal no fewer than thirty 'armed operations' against Africans for a year as late as 1915. After pacification, which was generally complete by about 1920, there followed the main central phase of the colonial period – *stagnation*. It engulfed all the colonial rulers, French, British, Belgian, Portuguese, Italian, and Spanish (for the Germans were out of the game by now). The 'period between the wars', 1919–39, was more often than not one of complete standstill except for a generally improved rate of profit on foreign mining operations. The colonial governments were left to live as best they could off the product of their own taxation; and this was so small that nothing but the bare minimum of administration could be paid for. Dismantlement continued.

The Second World War and its aftermath brought considerable change. With full employment in the western world, raw material prices boomed. Economic stagnation gave way to economic development; political repression began to retreat before the rise of a new nationalism. The continent began to heave and shift within itself. The 'sleepy giant', in Langston Hughes's affectionate phrase, was waking up at last.

In this sub-period after 1945 – the period of *struggle* – it is possible to argue that dismantlement stopped and reconstruction began. Perhaps so: yet one should be cautious at this point. As we shall see, the period of liberation inherited a major social crisis, and many of the elements in this crisis owed their origins, or at least their aggravation, to the years after 1945.

On the credit side there was notably a large expansion in the number of Africans who were able to win access to higher education. After 1945 'the new and significant development is the enormous increase in the number of students [who went from Africa to Western Europe]. ... Whereas their number is estimated to have been between 500 and 600 in 1939 [British colonies only], this had doubled by 1945, and had quadrupled by 1946. This sharp upward trend has continued, and on 1 January 1955, there were 10,000 colonial students in Britain, of whom 3,500 had arrived during 1954.'[22] French colonies experienced much the same growth.

But other colonies did not. The Portuguese (and Spanish) are once again at an extreme of negation. Only a few hundred nonwhites from the Portuguese African colonies have managed to climb into the university bracket during the last hundred years or so, and the position today is not significantly better (indeed, in some ways it is worse) than half a century ago. Nor is the situation significantly different at lower levels of education: the number of children at primary school in Angola and Moçambique is generally believed (in default of any detailed statistics) to constitute less than 1 per cent of the population, while the proportion at secondary school remains virtually invisible.

It could have been expected that a wealthy and industrially advanced country like Belgium would adopt a different approach. Yet, at the level of secondary and university education, the Belgian record is no better than the Portuguese, and may possibly be worse. Primary schooling (though with a heavy religious bias) reached a relatively high level in the Belgian Congo; semi-skilled and even skilled jobs were likewise open to African labourers. But even during their last years in the Congo the Belgians held firm to their earlier conviction that it would be wrong, because dangerous, to allow Africans to acquire any real knowledge of the outside world. Higher education in the Belgian Congo had produced fewer than a score of African graduates by the year in which the Belgians retired; in this vast country of peasant-farmers, there was only one Congolese graduate in agriculture.

This might have mattered less if higher education in Europe had been allowed to produce more. But the Belgian rulers took great care, and they were very careful people, to ensure that it should produce none at all. 'We have seen,' remarked a Belgian Minister of Colonies in 1954, 'that those natives who have been shown Europe, and given a very advanced education, do not always return to their homelands in a spirit favourable to civilization and to the Mother Country in particular.'[23]

It is accordingly not easy to perceive the constructive side of the Belgian colonial effort, even in the boom years after 1945. Its conductors could rightly claim to have ended the Arab-Swahili slave trade from the East Coast, together with the wretched internecine wars that had gone with it. Unfortunately, this useful achievement appears to have been at the cost, for other reasons, of no small proportion of the peoples concerned. Belgian rule had likewise opened roads, railways, and river communications; promoted mining industries, plantations, and even (latterly) a little manufacturing industry; and introduced millions of Africans to the spectacle of modern enterprise. Unhappily, though, the millions were all too often debarred from any real participation in the enterprise itself. The keynote of Belgian rule was paternalism; yet it was a kind of paternalism that seemed more than a little unwilling to see its 'children' on the road to maturity. None of this, needless to say, argues for a moment that Belgium was without her men of conscience and her administrators of high merit. But they were enmeshed in a system which could survive, it seemed, only in the absence of any genuine social, political, and economic advancement by the peoples of the country itself.

None of this, equally, argues that the Belgians were essentially much more wasteful or neglectful of human talent in Africa than their neighbours, the British and the French. Any Englishman who believes that the efforts of his countrymen have resolutely laid foundations for a new and modern society in Africa should consider the figures for primary and secondary education, no mean test of the rate of change and improvement in any society, African or not. Tanganyika passed under British authority in 1919. Forty years later, in 1959, its population had risen to nearly ten millions. And in 1959 the total number of secondary-school enrolments for Standard 12 (the last in the four-year secondary course) was 318, while the total number of School Certificates gained was 245. Kenya did a little better. Out of a population of some eight millions, 799 African boys and girls took School Certificate, and 654 achieved it. In Uganda, with a population of about six millions, as many as 860 African pupils won School Certificates in 1960. But adding these figures together, what do they reveal? That some 24 million people in British East Africa, after several decades of colonial rule, could together achieve an annual total of fewer than 2,000 School Certificates: less than one for every 12,000 of the population. It may be added that the university college of Makerere had 878 students in 1959, while the Royal College in Nairobi had 290; and even some of these came from outside East Africa.

Shortage of money? If this were a conclusive argument one would expect to see Northern Rhodesia, with enormous copper earnings every year, equipped with many secondary schools and even a university college. Yet in 1958 Northern Rhodesia, with more than two million Africans, possessed only one secondary school offering a complete course to the Senior Cambridge Certificate level. In Southern Rhodesia, likewise not lacking in revenue, figures for the same year of 1958 show that 12,148 African boys and girls entered school at the very bottom of the scale, in sub-standard A, but that those who reached the very top of the scale, standard 12, *numbered only thirteen*.[24]

Thus, while it is certainly true that in some respects (though not, it will be seen, in others) the process of dismantlement of traditional society slowed down after 1945, it is also true that the work of reconstruction scarcely began in the 'advanced colonies', and did not begin at all in the others.

In the wake of all this, with emotional judgements still reverberating through the whole firmament of debate, it is far from easy to summarize the outcome. There is no doubt that colonialism signalled a major upheaval in African life. And maybe the curious and contradictory nature of this upheaval can best be approached through a comparison with the industrial revolution of late-eighteenth- and early-nineteenth-century Britain. There, too, the change from one way of life to another took place through the violent and often blind destruction of traditional life and welfare, promoting great poverty and unprecedented rates of death and disease before producing, however slowly and reluctantly, a gentler and more expansive civilization, with reawakened social responsibility and, in the twentieth century, the beginnings of community development.

The colonial hurricane may be likened to that industrial transition. Both were the product of new pressures in world society with which the old ways were unable to coexist. Both were dedicated to an ideology of worldly individualist ambition. Both were hugely wasteful of human life and happiness. Both carried men away on a flood of dreams and nightmares, real enough at the time though reading strangely to us now. There is little point in lengthy moralizing. But just as it is clear today that the child labour and starvation of the English industrial revolution, with all the other horrors it entailed, were deplorably wasteful of human life and talent, so also may one now perceive that the colonial system, executing its work of dismantlement, was guilty of the same kind of waste and destruction.

There is another level of comparison as well. The whole outcome in Africa clearly turned, as it had turned in England, on
the degree in which the victims of the system could get to understand their situation, band together, and find ways of remoulding
it to their advantage, thus generalizing the benefits previously
available only to the ruling few. British efforts in that direction
make up Britain's social history for the last hundred years or
more. In Africa, a similar attempt dates from soon after the end
of the Second World War.

Not that Africa's movement of emancipation and self-enlarge-
ment, any more than Britain's, was without its long period of
ideological and political preparation. The African awakening
began with the plans and projects of men who had understood
the 'colonial situation' – and its challenge – not only in the
stagnating years of the twenties and thirties, but even before that
'situation' had fully taken shape.

There is no space here to examine how far this understanding
drew on memories of pre-colonial independence, and how far on
liberal or radical ideas arriving from the outside world. It seems
probable, for one, that the ideas animating the French revolution had more influence on certain parts of coastal Africa than
has been generally allowed. 'They have made,' wrote an angry
William Wilberforce in 1801 of the democratically obstructive
colonists of Sierra Leone, 'the worst possible subjects, as
thorough Jacobins as if they had been trained and educated in
Paris.'[25] But the memories of an older independence were always
potent. They echo firmly from the words of pioneering thinkers
like Horton, Blyden, and Hayford; and it is with these that any
serious estimation of the ideas animating African nationalism has
to begin.

4 Key Ideas

Many strands have gone into weaving the fabric of African nationalism, whether from native history or foreign example, devotion to high ideals or personal careerism, peace or war, hope or despair. We have glanced at some of them. Certainly, the list of 'foreign names' is long. The martyrs of Christianity are there; so are Rousseau and the Jacobins. Tom Paine is there; and Marx; Mazzini, and many lesser men.

Ideas of emancipation were transmitted and transposed in many ways and through many channels, most of them obscure. Egalitarian convictions reached by African troops on service outside their own countries during the two world wars are often said to have stood high on the list of pressures making for political change. Between 1914 and 1918, for example, more than 3,000 men of the Gold Coast Regiment served elsewhere. 'If they were good enough to fight and die in the Empire's cause,' declared the *Gold Coast Independent* in the wake of that war, 'they were good enough ... to have a share in the government of their countries.'[26]

It remains true, however, that the fabric was and is African, and that the dominating colours come from within the continent. One can see this even in the way in which general ideas discussed in other countries have acquired their African character.

Africa, in ages past, was the nursery of science and literature; from thence they were taught in Greece and Rome, so that it was said that the ancient Greeks represented their favourite goddess of Wisdom – Minerva – as an African princess ... Many eminent writers and historians agree that these ancient Ethiopians were Negroes ... And why should not the same race who governed Egypt ... who had her churches, her universities, and her repositories of learning and

47

science, once more stand on their legs and endeavour to raise their characters in the scale of the civilized world?[27]

These words of a Sierra Leonean doctor, J. Africanus Horton, written in *A Vindication of the African Race* published nearly a century ago, may or may not be good history: they strike in any case a very modern note. They sound the depth of modern African attitudes. And it is certainly true, in so far as it may matter in this context, that Herodotus was suggesting in the fifth century B.C. that the Egyptians were dark in colour and woolly of hair; that the Kushites (Horton's 'ancient Ethiopians') had invented their own alphabet, and were widely using it, by about 200 B.C., and that subsequent African peoples evolved highly literate variants of Islamic culture; while African forms of religion now appear, on less prejudiced inquiry, to be as spiritually respectable as other large systems of belief. So, in Horton's thinking – at the roots of African nationalism – old ideas combine with new, and unfamiliar thoughts with others which seem obvious.

The ideas of the African renaissance have a long and mixed pedigree. And a recognition of this is necessary to any consideration of the scope and nature of the slogans and programmes with which Africans have sought and found their political independence. It appears worth emphasizing that African nationalism is very far from being the sudden consequence of argument and action by what a former Chairman of the British South Africa Company described, in 1959, as 'a hard core of agitators and self-appointed leaders'. The 'hard core' theory can be argued only by those who are dishonest or politically inexperienced, for it is simply *not* how politics work. 'Agitators and self-appointed leaders' get nowhere unless they till well-prepared soil: let anyone who doubts this try pushing (no matter how 'hard') a Labour policy from door to door in a middle-class suburb, or, of course, the reverse.

The point is worth insisting on, perhaps, because many people still appear to think that African nationalism has been, and possibly still is, a minority phenomenon. Some people who think this do so in good faith: they tend in all honesty to interpret the actions and words of African leaders simply in reference to personal ambition, individual prejudice, or mere quirks of character. All these influences play their part, no doubt, but none of them matters beside the primary influence: the persistent pressure of popular opinion. Merely 'personal' interpretations of the African scene will obscure more than they reveal.

Others, it should be said, only pretend to believe that African nationalism is the work of a handful of agitators and self-appointed leaders. It is doubtful if the present rulers of South Africa actually hope that any reasonable person will accept their view of African nationalism as 'a communist plot'. Still, it does seem that many Europeans in Africa carefully harbour that illusion. Explaining how white civilization may yet be saved in Southern Rhodesia, a recent writer in that country urged that 'immediate action must be taken to counteract the virulent propaganda emanating from certain radio stations, notably Cairo. The mental poisoning pouring from these stations, if not countered, can have only disastrous effects.'[28] Countered, that is, not by social reforms calculated to remove grievances, but by radio-jamming and other censorship.

This line of thought, if that is what it can be called, is much followed by the Salazar regime in Portugal, where a Foreign Minister has lately claimed that the Portuguese colonies are 'confronted by the greatest conspiracy ever fabricated against any country'.[29] It may be that this politician actually believed what he wrote: the Portuguese rulers, after all, have dealt in conspiratorial politics for almost forty years. But that is no good reason for anyone else to believe it.

The key ideas of African nationalism are in fact neither new nor poor in parentage. Some of them are political in origin; others are religious. They all need to be kept in mind, however vaguely, when approaching the storms and battles of the past few years. 'Poor Resident,' wrote a Nyasaland African pastor *half a century* before Sir Roy Welensky and his associates were busy explaining the essentially 'communist' (and therefore, in Central Africa, quite new) nature of nationalism, 'he thinks too much of his skin and not of his heart. What is the difference between a white man and a black man? Are we not of the same blood and all from Adam? This startles me much – is Europe still Christian or Heathen? . . . If we had power enough to communicate ourselves to Europe we would advise them not to call themselves "Christendom" but "Europeandom". Therefore the life of the three combined bodies [Missionaries, Government, Companies] is altogether too cheaty, too thefty, too mockery. Instead of "Give" they say "Take away from".'[30]

There is one other preliminary point which seems important. Aderibigbe, a Nigerian historian, has lately complained that European writers have tended to overlook African resistance to the imposition of colonial rule, whereas for Africans, he says, the fact of resistance has been and still remains of great psychological significance.[31] And it is true that one can easily gain, from several recent historians, the impression that the colonial system was introduced more or less from one year to the next, or one decade to the next, with little more than 'local trouble' and, generally, to a great sigh of relief all round. Yet if others have tended to forget what really happened, Africans have evidently not. Even if they do not always or often know many of the facts, they know the legends of resistance; and the legends speak of long and exhausting struggle against invaders who came with fair words and stayed with foul. This memory of resistance adds its special flavour to African nationalism, giving it here and there an edge of bitterness that is otherwise attractively absent.

Not many documents have survived to record the African view of that struggle. But those which have invariably sound a note of pride and repudiation that also has its place in the genesis of current ideas. 'I have listened to your words,' an East African chief wrote in Swahili (the letter is fortunately preserved) to the German invader, von Wissmann, 'but can find no reason why I should obey you. . . . If it should be friendship that you desire, then I am ready for it, today and always; but to be your subject, that I cannot be . . .'[32]

This particular chief, as it happened, was also a slaver. No doubt it was right that his regime should go, as, in the course of fierce battles with the Germans, it eventually did. But the argument that the colonial regime occasionally imposed a better system on a worse is one that African nationalists have never found persuasive – a reluctance to see good in foreign domination that will surprise rather few people in the world today. And they have found it all the less persuasive because they have remembered their resistance. They have kept alive the names of many a hero who, like the brave Horatius admired so much by English schoolboys, died 'facing fearful odds, for the ashes of his fathers and the temples of his gods'. This attitude is likely, it seems, to persist. The more the colonial invasion recedes into the past, the more will Africans resurrect the epic of their struggles to resist it. In this, once again, they will of course be behaving, for better or for worse, like other peoples in other lands.

With these 'points of background' out of the way, we may now at last get down to considering what aspirations and intentions have moved the nationalism of Africa, and, after that, what success there has been in realizing them. Finally, it may then be possible to embark on some cautious prophecy about the future. If our approach has been rather slow and indirect, what follows will prove, I hope, all the more meaningful.

My first plan was to work to a regional scheme, for it is true that the key ideas of nationalism have a regional history and impact that are various and important. What happened in British West Africa was not the same as what happened in East Africa. The course of emancipation in the Congo was different from the growth of resistance in French territories. The Portuguese and Spanish colonies remain, to this day, in a daunting isolation of their own. . . . But the more I considered this plan of approach, the less satisfactory it promised to be. For it is also true that the ideas of African nationalism have acquired a continental validity (if within differing forms and fashions); that a regional approach would involve much irritating repetition; and that the influence of one region upon another constitutes a crucial aspect of the whole unfolding of events and programmes.

At some risk in over-simplification – but how avoid this, anyway? – I accordingly propose to look at recent African political experience under a few simple headings. These will cover the more important of the root-ideas now in play. First of all, there is a cluster of ideas which may be grouped as 'cultural and political': *nationalism* itself, *pan-africanism*, and *neutralism*, the last being linked in turn to notions of African particularity in the application or interpretation of general political concepts. Then there is a group of ideas which may be called 'economic and developmental': *neo-colonialism* and *African socialism* are typical of these. And of course there is over-lapping and interaction, so that a certain amount of repetition will be unavoidable. I shall try to keep this to a minimum.

5 Political Springboards

In Europe, at any rate, the word 'nationalism' has lately got itself – and how understandably! – a very bad name. It has generally come to represent a narrow-minded and backward-looking chauvinism: zenophobic, jealous, and at odds with the proper destiny of man. Yet this was not always so. This was not how nationalism appeared to the standard-bearers of Europe's 'submerged nationalities' a century ago. What they were fighting for was not the 'right to dominate' but the 'right to be free'. *This we swear, this we swear*, declaimed Hungary's great poet of the revolutionary year 1848, *slaves we will no longer be!*[33]

It may be, of course, that the nationalism of Africa will follow the same dismal road as the 'tribal nationalism' – to borrow Miss Hannah Arendt's telling phrase – of recent European history. That is one of the great unanswered questions of Africa's tomorrow. But for Africa today the dominant ideas of nationalism are still very much closer to those of the anti-imperialist movements of nineteenth-century Europe.

African Nationalism

The simple and straightforward demand for equality of rights has been, and is, as strong a motivation here as it ever was in Europe: stronger, perhaps, because the provocation has been so much more considerable. It would be hard to believe that the Hungarians of 1848 were 'slaves' to the Austrian Emperor in anything like the sense that vast numbers of Africans have been – and still, here and there, remain – slaves to other imperial masters. The first and greatest sense of African nationalism is the desire for personal emancipation.

An illuminating statement about this egalitarian meaning of

nationalism has lately come from a Southern Rhodesian (Zimbabwe) writer, Ndabaningi Sithole.

He is arguing with a white South African writer, Stuart Cloete. 'Let us have no illusions,' Cloete had written. 'The black man hates the white. Above all he hates him for being white, because this is something he can never be.'[34]

Nothing, Sithole replies, could be further from the truth:

On a purely human basis the African accepts the white man. In the majority of cases it is the white man who does not accept the African. One of the reasons why the white man fears granting the African full independence is that the African may use against the white man the hateful methods he has seen the white man use against the African.

What the African hates in the white man is his unfair social, economic, political, and educational discriminatory practices which relegate the African to second- or third-rate citizenship in the land of his birth. The African hates the white man's arrogance, his mania for humiliating him in the land of his birth . . . Politically, the white man dominates the African; economically, he exploits him; socially, he degrades his human status . . . It is these things that the African hates, and not the white man himself.

It is no accident, of course, that this statement should come from an African of Southern Rhodesia, where the whole white effort – whether masquerading as 'partnership' or declaring itself honestly as the means to an otherwise impossibly high minority income – has been to 'prove' that the black man is in fact an inferior kind of human being without any reasonable claim to a natural equality with the white. This claim is made more often and more emphatically, as you would expect, precisely in those territories of permanent white settlement where discrimination takes an ever-present, inescapable form. But it is also present elsewhere, if in muted tones, and this is because the whole of colonial Africa, in west or east, south or centre, has felt the same discrimination, has heard the same insistent declarations of natural white superiority.

This, too, is an aspect of the matter that tends to be forgotten. The claim to a natural superiority – and therefore to a 'right to dominate' – has come not only from white Rhodesian bars and clubs and their like, nor has it always been couched in the jargon of racial hatred and contempt that is customarily encountered in such places. The most respectable authorities have made this claim. 'In early life,' opined an eminent British anthropologist some seventy years ago, setting the tone for much that was to follow, Africans

evince a degree of intelligence which, compared with that of the European child, appears precocious; and they acquire knowledge with facility till they arrive at the age of puberty, when the physical nature masters the intellect, and frequently deadens it. This peculiarity, which has been observed amongst others of what are termed the lower races [he might have added, the lower classes too!], has been attributed by some physiologists to the early closing of the sutures of the cranium . . . They can imitate, but they cannot invent, or even apply. They constantly fail to grasp and to generalize a notion.[35]

A famous Victorian traveller, Sir Richard Burton, put the same idea more crudely. Once an African has become adult, he explained, 'his mental development is arrested, and thenceforth he grows backwards instead of forwards'. Exploded myths, no doubt; yet long-lived . . .

Meeting this kind of argument in his book of 1959, Sithole comes down to cases. 'There is no word here for "Thank you",' Cloete had written, 'for the people are without the concept that requires its use.' On the contrary, Sithole replies; and he proceeds to offer a short list of terms for 'thank you' in Ndebele, Shona, Luganda, Hausa, Tswana, and Sotho.

'The African,' Cloete had explained, 'has been conditioned by centuries of savage competition to seize what he desires wherever he can find it.' Anyone who knows anything of European history in the last hundred years (not to speak of earlier times) may wryly smile at Cloete's belief that Africans could be thought peculiar in this respect. Sithole makes the point.

We do not deny this . . . What concerns us here is the context in which [Cloete] makes this statement. He wants to give the false impression that it is *only* the African who has been so conditioned. We could reverse his statement so that it is equally applicable to any race in this world: namely, the European has been conditioned by centuries of savage competitive life to seize what he desires wherever he can find it. The occupation of Asia, Africa, the Americas, Australasia, and other non-European lands by Europeans is an historically irrefutable piece of evidence [to this effect] . . .

There is no need to follow Sithole further. The case is clear: nationalism in Africa today is primarily a claim for equality of status and of rights, for personal dignity, self-respect, full participation in the things of the material world as well as in the things of the spirit: a consistent effort to rescue Africans from their condition of acquired inferiority to which they have been relegated through the years. And this is everywhere true. The only real difference between regions is that the claim was heard in these terms a good deal earlier in West Africa than elsewhere. Nearly sixty years ago a Gold Coast (Ghanaian) writer recalled – with a relaxed note of laughter somewhat characteristic of his country – how he had argued with a certain European mining expert.

After he had spoken of *native* bush-path, *native* canoe, *native* river, *native* mines and *native* gold [wrote Mensah Sarbah], I asked him to explain to the court, in what respects *native* gold and the other native things particularly differed from those found in other parts of the world, but he could not; for the absurdity of always describing in Africa everything non-European as *native* had dawned on him by that time.[36]

'Native,' as we know, has long become a word so loaded with contempt in any part of English-speaking Africa as to be, merely by itself, a badge of supposed inferiority, not to say downright shame. I remember discussing this with an enlightened white trade unionist in South Africa some thirteen years ago. As a young woman she had made a tour of Europe, including the Soviet Union. 'Even then,' she recalled, 'I still regarded the natives as being pretty well sub-human. I remember they asked me in Russia if I was a native of the Union of South Africa; and I replied indignantly: "No, I'm a white woman, can't you see?"' Well, but this kind of thing gets tedious in the course of time; and African nationalism has abolished the word 'native' without feeling any further need for explanation.

Claims for equality of rights required clothing in political dress; and this soon took the necessary form of a demand for self-government. Here too, and for easily understood historical reasons, British West Africa led the way. (Early 'French African' claims were confused and therefore delayed by theories of assimilation and of French citizenship regardless of race, colour, or religion.) Not being colonies of settlement – differing sharply in this respect even from some of their French colonial neighbours – Nigeria, Ghana, and Sierra Leone (with the Gambia adding a minor harmony in the background) had early acquired at least the embryonic institutions of representative government.

In 1844 a dozen Fanti chiefs in the Gold Coast had agreed in certain circumstances to recognize the authority of British criminal law, and this *Bond* became a symbol of the political autonomy of African chiefs within their range of authority – as well, of course, as a recognition of British rule. But 1852 brought the creation of a legislative assembly in the territory, and although this proved abortive, it set men thinking. The movement towards self-government was slow and uncertain, and was obstructed by British policy more often than it was encouraged; but 1888 none the less saw the nomination – democratic election being still far ahead – of an African to membership of the legislative council. In 1894 there came the establishment of three municipal councils; and gradually it became clear, as the years slowly succeeded each other, that representative government for the whole country could be permanently withheld only by force. Yet not until after 1945 did the threat of force begin to appear difficult and undesirable for Britain to apply. Developments in Lagos and the southerly parts of Nigeria followed much the same lines.

Nationalism, as such, appeared in full array during the First World War. There emerged the National Congress of British West Africa and other bodies to the same general effect. Names began to be heard that were soon famous. One of them was that of Joseph Ephraim Caseley Hayford. Speaking at Freetown in 1920, this Gold Coast journalist traced, for the whole of British West Africa, a programme whose wider meaning we can easily recognize today. 'We have passed the childhood stage,' Hayford declared on that occasion, 'and much as we appreciate the concern of our guardians, the time has come for us to take an intelligent active part in the guiding of our own national destiny; and that is the primary fact that has called into being the National Congress of British West Africa.'[37]

The terms seem old-fashioned and Uncle-Tom-like today; but when they were used they sounded subversive in many ears. The *national* note was firmly struck, if still in a vaguely regional context, and for reasons that were perfectly clear to the men of that time. To far-seeing men of colour these reasons had long been clear. 'The claims of no people,' an American Negro leader, Martin Delany, had argued as early as 1852, 'are respected by any nation until they are presented in a national capacity.'[38] This indeed may yet prove to have been Europe's major contribution to African politics: the conviction that progress and equality were possible only at the price of 'nationhood' – even though the concept of exclusivist nationalism was one which fitted the African situation even less hopefully than any other.

Become nations: or you cannot become free. In some such imperative as this the European message reached African ears, decade after decade, through a multitude of more or less sceptical exhortations. A people without nationalism was said to be a people without history, and a people without history could have no identity, and therefore no real claim on that dignity and self-respect which even the poorest European peoples had successfully acquired for themselves. The lesson was to be well learned.

So it came about that Africans, more and more, found themselves impelled to demand their freedom within ideological boundaries which seemed right and natural to their European rulers – the kind of boundaries within which the peoples of Europe had gained their own independence. The notion that freedom could be possible and even preferable within supra-national boundaries or by means of supra-national or even continental institutions was impossibly far ahead at the time; and, as we well know, to a large extent still is so. Whether regionalist and 'unitarian' solutions are to remain impossible, however, is already a significant part of the ideological conflict in Africa at this moment, a point to which we shall return later.

Having posed their demands within a narrowly national framework – even though this often represented multi-national or supra-national realities, as notably in Nigeria – African leaders pressed them. The years of the late twenties and thirties – of what I have called the phase of stagnation – offered, however, only repression in return. Little was achieved. But the Second World War, fought most consciously against the ideology of racism represented by the German Nazis and Italian Fascists, proved a great liberator. Sithole has a wry and telling tale to this effect.

'Away with Hitler! Down with him!' said the British officer [appealing for Africans to fight against Hitler].
'What's wrong with Hitler?' asked the African.
'He wants to rule the whole world,' said the British officer.
'What's wrong with that?'
'He is German, you see,' said the British officer, trying to appeal subtly to the African's tribal consciousness.
'What's wrong with his being German?'
'You see,' said the British officer, trying to explain in terms that would be conceivable to the African mind, 'it is not good for one tribe to rule another. Each tribe must rule itself. That's only fair. A German must rule Germans, an Italian, Italians, and a Frenchman, French people.'[39]

The point was taken. African nationalism came of age during this war. By 1944 powerful new notes were sounding up and down the continent. The old Uncle-Tom-ism vanished from the scene. What was felt now was not 'appreciation for the concern of our guardians,' but growing impatience with any claim that these guardians had ever played a useful purpose.

'We who live in this blessed country of Nigeria,' wrote Nnamdi Azikiwe, one of the outstanding pioneers of West African nationalism, just sixteen years before his country became independent, 'know that until we are in control of political power in our country we would continue to be the footstool of imperialist nations, who are interested selfishly in their economic prosperity and social prestige. ... If there is any doubt about the yearnings of Nigerians for self-government, it should be dispelled forthwith. We are fed up with being governed as a Crown Colony, which we are N O T. We are nauseated by the existence of an untrammelled bureaucracy which makes, administers, and interprets our laws, without our knowledge and consent. The idea of our paid civil servants ruling and lording it over us is a challenge to our manhood, both as a nation and as a race.'[40]

The blessed country of Nigeria, of course, contained several peoples whose right to consider themselves as nations, even within the narrowest meaning of the term, was obvious to anyone who had thought about the matter. But the need for a nationalist framework was understood even where peoples had generally lived without it, or without more than a primitive sense of it. 'National union is necessary,' ran a Congolese manifesto in 1956, 'because the whole population [of the Belgian Congo] must now accept a national character and the unity that flows from it. ... We are convinced that it is perfectly possible for Catholics, Protestants, Salvation Army-ists, [*Salutistes,*] and Muslims to agree on a programme for their common good such as respects the principles of natural morality engraved in the hearts of all men worthy of the name ...'[41]

Such arguments were widely accepted. When the French in 1959 and 1960 finally withdrew their political control from their West and Equatorial African dependencies, it appeared natural that the administrative units in question should become as many separate states. Besides, peoples long suppressed were eager to stand forth in the world with an acknowledged identity of their own. All the same, it is worth recalling in this connexion that there were efforts to transpose the colonialist federal structures of French West Africa and Equatorial Africa (eight and four units respectively) into independent federal structures; and the full record, when it becomes available, may yet show that these efforts could have succeeded if governments in Paris had cared actively to help them.*

For even in the full surge of nationalism during the fifties there were not lacking men who said that *federal structures*, and not a maze of little separate states, ought to follow the colonial partition. Nigeria was fortunate in this respect. The eight territories of French West Africa might well have repeated Nigeria's example. There were men in East Africa who already argued that the road of 'balkanization' must quickly take them to disaster.

* Ironically, it was the *Loi Cadre* of the Fourth Republic which, while opening the way to territorial independence, largely ruined the hope of territorial federation.

The same note was struck in the central-southern regions
This underlying thought belonged to another of nationalist
Africa's basic group of ideas.

Pan-Africanism

It might have been expected that the ideas expressed by Pan-
Africanism would evaporate with the coming of political independence to most of Africa. For they were initially the ideas of
the Negro diaspora beyond the Atlantic. They spoke for the
dream of those many men and women of African descent who,
finding themselves in the midst of white American cultures
which rejected them, reacted by looking back across the ocean
for a new integration of their lives and hopes. 'Black Africa,' in
the well-known words of the Martinique poet, Aimé Césaire,
'is the mother of our West Indian civilization, and it is she who
will regenerate our energy and hope. . . .'

Another poet, Claud McKay, has put it this way:

> For the dim regions whence my fathers came
> My spirit, bondaged by the body, longs.
> Words felt, but never heard, my lips would frame;
> My soul would sing forgotten jungle songs.
> I would go back to darkness and to peace.
> But the great western world holds me in fee,
> And I may never hope for full release
> While to its alien gods I bend my knee . . .[42]

Not only that: there was also the belief that a free Africa could
help to liberate the Negroes oversea. 'It may be that the day is
not far off,' a Negro American had written in the *New York Age*
in 1923, 'when the new Negroes of Africa will be demanding
that their blood brothers in the United States be treated with
absolute fairness and justice.' An extravagant fancy when it was
written: yet in 1963 a conference of African students from
twenty-six countries expressed their solidarity 'with Negro
students fighting for equality in the United States of America'.[43]

At the root of these mainly transatlantic ideas about Pan-
Africanism or Pan-Negroism, there lay the dual notion of Negro
rights and of 'Africa for the Africans'. How completely this was
so may be seen in the first Pan-African Congress ever held.

61

Organized in 1900 by a Trinidad barrister, H. Sylvester Williams, it gave a platform to another figure who would become much better known, W. E. B. DuBois. These men looked across to Africa with a bitter awareness of their own unity in disfranchisement: here in the New World all Africans had lost their separate ethnic loyalties, languages, cultures, sense of difference from one another;* and so it appeared natural to regard all Africans as belonging to the same great territorial unit, Africa, however much that unit might be divided within itself by 'the frontiers of foreign rule'. This visionary attitude induced an illumination that was to seem prophetic in later years, for it was during this first Pan-African Congress that DuBois threw down his famous challenge. 'The problem of the twentieth century,' he declared in the year of its birth, and with colonial conquest in full assault, 'is the problem of the colour line – the relation of the darker to the lighter races of men in Asia and Africa, in America and the islands of the sea.'

The Pan-Africanists were naturally ignored by the busy imperialist world. They were few, and they seemed to have no influence. But they went on hammering at their theme. Christian Negro missionaries began exporting their ideas into the heart of Africa.[44] Political journalists began reflecting and developing them on the West Coast. In 1919 a second congress met, this time in Paris where the victorious Powers of the First World War were deciding how they should settle the peace. Fifty-seven delegates were present: 'Negroes in the trim uniform of American army officers,' an American newspaper reported at the time, 'coloured men in frock coats or business suits, polished French Negroes who hold public offices. . . .'[45]

The delegates boldly addressed themselves to the Powers. They called on them to 'establish a code of law for the international protection of the natives of Africa, similar to the proposed international code for labour', and laid down a list of 'principles' by which 'the natives of Africa and the peoples of African descent' should henceforth be governed. We are still, it will be seen, at a relatively early stage of the argument: outright

* There were corners of the New World where the descendants of transported Africans had clung to some of their old ways and languages. But these cases were marginal; they do not affect the argument here.

demands for self-government and independence seemed hope-lessly premature, as indeed they undoubtedly would have been. The colonial Powers were still engaged in 'pacifying' their newly won subjects in Africa: the notion that they should now pack their bags and leave would have struck them, even if they had deigned to notice it, as absurd.

Yet these demands of the second congress pointed forward to a steady crystallization of new ideas. They were Pan-African, and they were libertarian. Moreover, and the influence of DuBois counted for much in this, they gave due weight to the customs and beliefs of pre-colonial Africa – to all that complex of tradition which had carried Africans through the years before conquest. They affirmed:

> The land and its natural resources should be held in trust for the natives.... The investment of capital and granting of concessions should be so regulated as to prevent the spoliation of the natives and the exhaustion of natural wealth. ... Slavery and corporal punishment should be abolished and forced labour except in punishment of crime. ... It should be the right of every native child to learn and write his own language, and the language of the trustee nation, at public expense. ... And the natives of Africa should have the right to participate in government as fast as their development might permit. ...[46]

During and after the Second World War these ideas and others like them became common coinage among youthful nationalists in Africa; and now they were rephrased for a specifically African context. In this respect the sixth congress, held at Manchester in 1945, was crucial. Here for the first time the Old Guard from over the ocean was flanked by new men from the continent itself: obscure young men, for the most part, whom few in England (or anywhere else) had ever heard of – among them Kenyatta from Kenya, Nkrumah from the Gold Coast, Akintola from Nigeria, Johnson from Sierra Leone. The old notion of 'European trusteeship' went neck and crop out of the window into the Manchester fog. 'We demand for Africa,' the delegates resolved, 'autonomy and independence, so far, and no further, than it is possible in this One World for groups and peoples to rule themselves subject to inevitable world unity and federation.'

The language was unambiguous in spite of a romantic bow in

the direction of 'world unity'. It offered a new tune to the brief
harmony of worldwide victory over racism. To grasp the hopes
of that meeting one must recall the scene in India at the time, for
India was then moving rapidly towards independence under
pressure from the militant Congress movement, and the British
Labour Party, just elected to power, was known to favour that
cause. If India could be free, why not Africa? There was ground
for a new hopefulness. Meanwhile the Pan-Africanists in Manchester restricted themselves to a threat of what might have to
happen if Africa's legitimate ambitions should continue to be
thrust aside. 'We are determined to be free,' they said, '[but]
if the Western world is still determined to rule Mankind by force,
then Africans, *as a last resort*, may have to appeal to force in the
effort to achieve freedom. . . .' It was the first time that Africa's
challenge would be posed in this form. Later years would
see it realized in North Africa, in the Portuguese colonies, and
elsewhere on the continent.

The ideas of Pan-Africanism, though budded outside Africa,
were not allowed to wither with the coming of independence.
So little were these ideas forgotten, indeed, that they may even
be said to have presided over the 'great year of independence',
1960, when no fewer than sixteen African colonies won their
sovereignty.

The historical facts are that a multitude of colonies became
independent states; that constitutional declarations in favour of
federal union went for little or nothing; that the one coherent
effort at securing such a union – between the former colonies of
Senegal and Soudan – fell apart almost at once;* and that unity
movements soon took the merely diplomatic and tactical form
of 'bloc alliances' named after the capitals where they were
formed, such as Casablanca, Monrovia, and Brazzaville. Yet it is
also true that the ideal of continental unity was enshrined during
this formative period as one of the guarantees, perhaps the
fundamental guarantee, of true development and progress. With
a startling impact on large numbers of men and women, there
suddenly appeared the prospect of an African civilization into
which all the many different streams of African thought,

* The Federation of Mali, formed on 17 January 1959 and dissolved on 1 August
1960.

experience, and resource should flow, fortifying the belief that these peoples could thus achieve a place and weight in the world commensurate with their continent.

There was plenty of ground for scepticism. Africa remained full of more or less bitter internecine conflicts and potential frontier wars. The large capitals of the world flew a score and more of African flags on separate (and separately very costly) embassies and missions; and each of these represented a network of individual interests and careers. The old sores of tribalism began to reopen and fester. A little country like Kenya, weighed down with poverty and unemployment, was expected to take its final steps to independence as a cluster of petty statelets loosely connected to a central government. Other newly independent states threatened to go the same way. Yet the ideas of unity stubbornly remained, and remain, near the centre of the picture. The vision still glitters, still beckons.

The astonishing persistence of the idea of a Congolese nation, in the face of every obstacle and provocation to the contrary, is perhaps the most convincing token of the power in that vision. As another token, here is a summary of resolutions passed by a conference of delegates from twenty-six African student unions in Europe and America when they met in London in April 1963. These resolutions are important not only for what they say but also for who composed them. Many crucial jobs will be filled in Africa from the ranks of these delegates during the next few years:

Instruments giving expression to African Unity [should] be created as a matter of urgency. . . . A method of political coordination [should] be worked out in the consolidating of African Unity. . . . A Political Constitution applying throughout the continent [should] be formulated and accepted. . . . This Political Constitution should make provision for the establishment of a Pan-African Parliament, a Pan-African Executive and Public Service. . . . A Pan-African Army under joint high command [should] be created from national contingents in order to safeguard the integrity of the African continent. . . .

This Pan-African Army is urgently needed in order to defend Africa against continuing aggression in South Africa, Angola, Portuguese Guinea, Moçambique, and other areas temporarily under colonial subjection. . . .

Africa should be free of all foreign military bases, nuclear and atomic testing facilities, and foreign military missions or pacts. . . . The foreign policy of African countries should in any case be guided only by the principles of a most rigorous positive neutralism. . . . African countries must therefore free themselves from partnership in any foreign national groupings which are not compatible with African positive neutralism. . . .

That these were not isolated voices, mere student romantics rebelling against the established trend of orthodox opinion in their homelands, was shown by the African Unity Conference of thirty-two independent countries (all except two, Morocco and Togo, represented by their heads of state) which gathered at Addis Ababa in May 1963. There, a charter for African unity was drawn up and accepted. An Organization for African Unity was formed, providing for an assembly of heads of state or government to meet at least once a year, a council of ministers to meet at least twice a year, a secretariat (to be situated in Addis Ababa), and a commission for mediation, conciliation, and arbitration.* With this, the organic concept of political and economic unity in Africa was clearly on the map.

Much of the drive behind the Addis conference was undoubtedly due to President Nkrumah of Ghana. The 'ideas of Manchester' had remained with him. He saluted Ghana's independence in 1957 by roundly declaring that the achievement would be meaningless unless it helped towards the liberation of the whole continent. With that in mind, Nkrumah early set about promoting unity of action. When French Guinea became independent in October 1958 he made available to President Sékou Touré a loan of £10 millions (other loans of £4 to £5 millions each were later advanced to Mali and Upper Volta, as well as many lesser sums to nationalists up and down the continent) and, a month later, concluded a Ghana–Guinea 'union' which was intended 'to form a nucleus for a Union of African States'.[47] A month later again an All-African People's Conference at Accra gathered delegates from sixty-two nationalist organizations. In July 1959 Nkrumah went to Saniquellie, in Liberia, for unity discussions with Presidents Tubman and Touré; in December 1960, with Touré and President Kéita of Mali (now severed from Senegal), he formed a Ghana–Guinea–

* See On the Record, p. 183.

Mali Union. This was named 'the Union of African States and was to form a nucleus of the United States of Africa'.[48] In January 1961 these three states met at Casablanca with the leaders of Egypt, Morocco, and the Algerian Front de Libération Nationale (F.L.N.), as well as a representative of the Libyan government, and established a consultative assembly together with other coordinating instruments.

None of this escaped sharp criticism and opposition from other African states. Nigeria led another grouping – known as the Monrovia Bloc after the Liberian capital where it first met – while many former French colonies had a separate 'organization' of their own, known as the Brazzaville Bloc, with President Houphouët-Boigny of the Ivory Coast in the lead.

Yet these various and often acutely opposed groupings all met at the Addis conference where, at last, they made some progress towards unification of *overall* policy and objective. If much of the running continued to be made by Ghana, the final pace was set by Nigeria and like-minded 'moderates', including Liberia and Ethiopia, who all put forward detailed plans for varying methods of securing common action and agreement. It was the government of the Sudan, for instance, which pressed that Africa should become a zone free of nuclear weapons and foreign pacts. The conference was rightly hailed as a success. It had achieved much more than the many sceptics had believed possible.

It was certainly helped by finding a common enemy in the continued white domination of southern Africa – whether by the South African National Party under Dr Verwoerd or by the agents of the Portuguese dictator, Salazar, or by the settlers of Southern Rhodesia. Looking back, though, one can see that opinion had moved a long way since the eve of 'independence year', 1960. Reacting then to Ghanaian propaganda for unity, the Federal Prime Minister of Nigeria, Sir Abubakar Tafawa Balewa, had voiced a widespread attitude when declaring, in January 1960: 'A United States of Africa? Oh, surely it is very premature to start talking about anything like that. Nigeria has not the slightest intention of surrendering her sovereignty, no sooner has she gained her independence, to anyone else, including other West African countries.'[49]

In 1963 the idea of a full-blown United States of Africa, vigorously sponsored by Nkrumah, was evidently still 'very premature'; but the suspicion that such an idea was somehow part of a 'Ghanaian plot' had disappeared (or at any rate much faded), and several steps towards a supra-national organization of African states had actually been taken – with the Nigerian government's active sponsorship and participation. Moreover, programmes for regional unity looked like making real progress in British East Africa, where three former colonies, Tanganyika, Uganda, and Kenya (the last not yet quite independent) met in June 1963 to consider practical steps towards federal union.

The real lines of division had in fact significantly shifted. At the Addis conference these were no longer between 'Casablanca' and 'Monrovia', between the 'left-wing' states and the 'moderates'; and they had likewise moved from the familiar Ghana–Nigeria deadlock towards a new pattern. This new pattern tended, though latently as yet, to assemble the genuinely independent leaders (whether 'left-wing' or 'moderate') on one side, leaving the much-less-than-genuinely-independent spokesmen of the Brazzaville grouping on the other. Apart from the Ivory Coast and Madagascar, relatively large and rich, these 'Brazzaville' states were a scattering of little former French colonies whose dependence on France, whether directly through financial and other ties or indirectly through 'association' with the West European Common Market, was often described as 'semi-colonial'.

How far this description might be justified could be measured to some extent by the number of French troops stationed in the ex-colonies of West and Equatorial Africa and Madagascar: early in 1963 they still attained the remarkable total of 20,000. The presence of these French troops, together with French advisers and administrators, was in line with defence agreements signed with France by all these territories except Guinea and Mali, agreements which provided for bilateral defence planning and the installation of permanent French military establishments. They cost France £68 millions in 1963.

It was hard to see how such agreements could be compatible with a full development of local sovereignty. 'One of the key clauses in each of the agreements,' *West Africa* remarked on

24 August 1963, after the brief intervention and withdrawal of French troops in defence and then abandonment of Fulbert Youlou in Congo (Brazzaville), 'is that which allows African governments to appeal to French armed forces to assume the "maintenance of the organization of their own armies". . . . In response to such an appeal, France may "intervene directly" in the African state. . . . France also has special agreements with most of her African ex-colonies to deal with the participation of French armed forces in the maintenance of public order . . . Although these particular agreements remain secret, they appear to provide for the indigenous government to call upon French troops to intervene in case of a threat to peace and public order. The call may be refused, and must anyway be approved by a decision of the French cabinet.' Thus France retains much indirect and even direct political and military power in most of her former African territories. The distance between these French Community agreements and the British Commonwealth framework may be seen by comparing their impact and implications with what has happened in Nigeria. There the mere acquisition of British military air-staging rights has failed to withstand Nigerian opposition.

It was clearly with these 'Brazzaville states' in mind, tied so closely and even exclusively to France and the West European Common Market, that Nkrumah at the Addis conference hammered home his theme that 'Africa must unite or perish', called for 'common functional organs', and argued that 'it should be possible to devise some constitutional structure which secures these objectives and yet preserves the sovereignty of each country joining the Union'. Only an Africa free to develop its vast potential without hampering restrictions by the old colonial Powers could properly advance the interests of its several parts. Only an Africa with a centralized political direction could successfully give effective material and moral support to Africans not yet free.

So many blessings must flow from our unity; so many disasters must follow on our continued disunity. . . .

It is said, of course, that we have no capital, no industrial skill, no communications and no internal markets, and that we cannot even agree among ourselves how best to utilize our resources. Yet all the stock exchanges of the world are preoccupied with Africa's gold, diamonds, uranium, platinum, copper, and iron ores. Our capital flows out in streams to irrigate the whole system of Western economy. Fifty-two per cent of the gold in Fort Knox at this moment, where the U.S. stores its bullion, is believed to have originated from our shores. . . .

Proposals for an African Common Market drew the same kind of arguments in its support. Not long after the Addis conference the United Africa Company (a dependent of Unilever) opened in Ghana a plant to manufacture 24,000 tons of soap a year, as well as toothpaste and related products. Speaking on this occasion, Nkrumah pointed out that the factory was no larger not because Unilever could not afford a much bigger one, but because there was an insufficiently large market. 'Many African states,' he went on, 'still impose customs duties and import restrictions originally designed to limit the trade of the colony in the interest of the manufacturing industries of the imperial power.' If they had factories, these were small, 'and the price of our manufactured goods is far higher than it need be if there was a larger market'. The foreign investor suffered no less. His 'vested interest in African unity is as great as that of any African today'.

Whatever his fellow-leaders at Addis may have thought of Nkrumah's words, the larger fact remained that the nationalism of a major part of Africa would now appear to have turned – even in spite of separatist agreements linked to the 'protection area' of the West European Common Market – away from small-nation isolationism along familiar lines and towards the concept of continental integration. It is perfectly evident from the present scene that the difficulties in actually realizing this objective, or any serious aspect of it, will be many, stubborn, and opaque. These difficulties may very possibly prevail. What we can note today is that a large number of African peoples, including some of the most dynamic and least poor, are much concerned with unity. This may be one of the most telling if least observed factors of international life today.

The reasons for this trend are complicated. Pan-Africanist propaganda could never have made headway against the fervent pressures of small-nation separatism unless its teachings had fallen on fertile ground. Part of this ground lay in the common formation of Africa's leaders. (Many of ex-French West Africa's leading intellectuals, for example, got to know each other, discussed the same ideas, and nursed the same hopes, at the William Ponty *lycée* in Dakar.) A larger part lay in the manifest truth that nearly all of Africa occupied the same political and economic position in relation to the rest of the world, and shared the same basic problems. But still another part, and not the least, lay in what may be called a growing sense of 'one-ness', of 'Africanness', of possessing the same fundamental scale of values and beliefs, a scale which formed an 'identity' that was specifically African, a 'personality' that should now, in the wake of colonial subjection, find its full and public expression.

The African Personality

If I went to heaven, and God said, 'Aggrey, I am going to send you back, would you like to go as a white man?' I should reply, 'No, send me back as a black man, yes, completely black.' And if God should ask, 'Why?' I would reply, 'Because I have a work to do as a black man that no white man can do. Please send me back as black as you can make me.' . . . I am proud of my colour: whoever is not proud of his colour is not fit to live.[50]

That was forty years ago, and the confidence for which Aggrey spoke was part and parcel of the West African nationalist movement. But the characteristic writings of Négritude belong to the poets of the Caribbean and their French-speaking African friends in the Paris of the nineteen-forties and fifties, although it was actually in 1939 that Césaire had 'founded the movement' with his *Cahiers d'un retour au pays natal* (*Notes on Going Home*). As with Pan-Africanism, Négritude with them was a means of protest, a weapon in the struggle for equality of status, a challenge cast in the face of a world which appeared to worship mere material achievement.

Romantic, 'political' only by implication, even metaphysical, Négritude was the mantle of culture within which deprived and despised peoples should now regain their birthright. 'Only Africa,' in Césaire's words, 'can revitalize, repersonalize the West Indies.' But Africa had first to 'repersonalize' herself, move out from under the shadow of Europe and display her own

71

virtues to her own delight, show the world that she too was an integral and inseparable part of humanity's achievement and endeavour:

> For it is not true at all that the work of man is finished
> that we have nothing more to do in the world
> that it is enough that we should set ourselves in the steps
> of the world
> but the work of man is only beginning . . .
> and no race possesses the monopoly of beauty intelligence
> force
> and there is room for all of us at the rendezvous of
> victory.[51]

These ideas excited the intellectuals of all those African countries faced with European policies of cultural assimilation. Many followed Césaire's trumpet call. Brilliant among them was the young Léopold Senghor, now President of Senegal, whose poetry most dramatically displays the schismic clash between 'becoming a Frenchman' and 'remaining an African', and resolves it – at any rate in verse – in favour of the second.

Senghor strode the pavements of the white man's world and sang their misery and solitude, longing for the 'joy and community' of his homeland, as in his poem *New York*, where white Manhattan and black Harlem are compared with one another:

> No mother's breast, but only nylon legs. Legs and breasts
> that have no sweat nor smell,
> No tender word for there are no lips, only artificial
> hearts paid for in hard cash.
> Nights of insomnia or nights of Manhattan . . .
> Harlem! Harlem! Harlem! Now I saw Harlem! A
> green breeze of corn springs up from
> the pavements ploughed by
> the naked feet of dancers,
> Bottoms waves of silk and sword blade breasts, water-lily
> ballets and fabulous masks . . .[52]

The note was a new one from an African, but not unique. 'I feel ridiculous,' sang Léon Damas,

> in their shoes, in their dinner jackets
> in their stiff shirts, their paper collars,

> with their monocles and bowler hats
> I feel ridiculous
> with my toes that were not made
> to sweat from morning to evening
> in their swaddling clothes that weaken my limbs
> and deprive my body of its beauty.[53]

It passed from the French-speaking poets to those who wrote in English. 'Then I came back,' remembered Abioseh Nicol of Sierra Leone, 'sailing down the Guinea coast':

> Go up-country, they said,
> To see the real Africa.
> For whomsoever you may be,
> That is where you come from.
> Go for bush – inside the bush
> You will find your hidden heart,
> Your mute ancestral spirit.
>
> And so I went,
> Dancing on my way.[54]

It acquired a more clearly political accent, reaching out towards a conflict of cultures and policies and programmes, as in these lines by the Ghanaian Dei-Anang:

> Here we stand
> Poised between two civilizations
> Backward? To days of drum
> And festal dances in the shade
> Of sun-kist palms.
> Or forward?
> Forward!
> Toward?
> The slums, where man is dumped upon man? . . .[55]

It moved across the continent. It was heard and echoed back in remote places, as in this statement of defiant hope by the Kimbundu poet of Angola, Agostinho Neto:

> My mother (black mother whose sons depart)
> you taught me to wait and hope
> as you had learnt in bitter days
>
> But in me
> life killed that mystic hope

73

> I am not the one who waits
> but the one who is awaited
> And we are Hope
> your sons ...
> searching for life.[56]

Négritude 'naturalized itself': in so doing, it lost much of its racialist undertone and stood forth as a statement about people, people who happened to be African. But all this – and the poetry of the African renaissance became a flood in these years of self-realization and self-questioning – struck at the artists with peculiar force. They were involved in national movements impatient of the traditional past, the past that had delivered them into colonial subjection; and yet the idiom of a new and different future seemed repeatedly to lead them back only to European forms and motives that spelt imitation – and therefore disaster for any true growth of the arts. Which path could they follow?

Beier has commented:

The Nigerian artist finds himself between two groups of people: enthusiastic Europeans, many of whom want him to be exotic and who want to recognize in his work clever adaptations of traditional motifs. On the other hand there is the Nigerian middle class, who are not very interested in his activities but who certainly do *not* want to be reminded in any way of traditional art, which is a world they feel they have left behind them, and in which they do not recognize any lasting values.[57]

The artistic dilemma is thus a real one, and will not soon be resolved. But it is variously posed. Very differently, for example, in South Africa. The protest and political inwardness of Négritude consisted precisely in its denial of assimilation – because assimilation meant acceptance of Africans (or West Indians) only at the price of becoming 'honorary whites'. But in South Africa Africans were offered 'acceptance' (the inverted commas are very necessary) only if they remained *outside* the pale of white civilization – which meant, in the circumstances of South Africa, denial of any real access to the modern world. Apartheid, 'separate development', promised nothing but a permanent deprivation of dignity and manhood.

Reacting against this, African writers in South Africa have proclaimed what may be called the indivisibility of culture. For them, Négritude and its accent on African-ness seemed only to be playing into the hands of white communities whose own policy was based on a reversal of the same conception. They have consequently tended to condemn Négritude as a kind of racialism, and in doing so they have found justification in the more extreme forms of Negro protest now appearing in the United States, among for instance the 'Black Moslems' who seem to have elevated the older 'Back to Africa' ideas of Marcus Garvey and others into a fanatical creed of racialist exclusivism. 'To us in multi-racial communities,' the South African Ezekiel Mphahlele has remarked in an illuminating commentary, 'Négritude is just so much intellectual talk, a cult.'[58]

Mphahlele believes that a new art in Africa will arise from the stuff of life itself, and not from any cult of particularity, separateness, or racial difference. At the back of his thought there lies the memory and knowledge of the way in which Africans of his own country, grappling with the squalid superficialities of white culture which are all that is 'allowed them', have none the less succeeded time after time in creating valid works of art, whether in music, painting, or literature. He is impatient with the solitary souls who try 'reintegration' in condescending Paris or London. 'The number of African artists and writers who have not been discovered, because they are locked up in their ghettoes in multi-racial communities, and who cannot speak to a world audience because of brutal white rule and racial prejudice, is much too large compared with the few who go abroad – too large for us to worry excessively about the latter.' It is one of the historical achievements of Africans in South Africa to have raised the ideal of non-racialist humanism above the muck and misery of apartheid. And one may well believe that it is one of Africa's major tragedies that these very Africans should be sealed off behind barricaded frontiers during the crucial years of continental search for a common future.

But Négritude, in 'naturalizing itself', became part of a larger and more emotive theme. 'My country groans,' in Azikiwe's words, 'under a system which makes it impossible for us to develop our personalities to the full.'[59] What did he really mean? In answering this question we encounter the ideological projection of the political and programmatic slogans of the past ten years and more. With the idea of 'the African personality', nationalist politics took a new and original turn. 'National liberation' became identified with 'African liberation'. The claims of Pan-Africanism acquired a philosophical justification.

The thought expressed in Azikiwe's words was given a continental framework. It was right to liberate the peoples of Africa because they could not otherwise enjoy their own separate identities – but also because they could not otherwise develop that special attitude and temperament by which Africa, within her multitude of variations, displays her inner unity, her 'personality' that is ultimately unique, distinct, and comprehensive.

To some extent this proclamation of 'an underlying African cultural unity' may be a mere response to the familiar European proposition – that nothing but colonial rule has ever united Africans. 'The only common factor in the heterogeneous tribes of Africa,' according to a recent and characteristic European statement of this sort, 'is the human form.'[60] This kind of attitude is considered profoundly offensive by educated Africans today not so much, it seems, for its splenetic condescension as for its denial of any political basis for unity. For if it were true that the many peoples of Africa are nothing more than a scatter of unrelated or even fundamentally opposed units, then clearly the fate of these units must lie in the slow crystallization of nation-states whose individual weakness or ambition can never hope to save them, at least for long into the future, from the tutelage of foreign masters, or else from wars of conquest such as the records of European nation-states have abundantly illustrated. But is the independence of Africa to be merely a prelude to anything as unpromising as that? The ideologists of Africa today have generally revolted against any such prospect. 'On the contrary,' they tend to reply, 'we shall build our future on the basis of an underlying cultural unity which, in fact, really does relate most of our peoples to the same body of ideas.'

What 'underlying cultural unity'? What 'body of ideas'? We shall take a look at the political answers – neutralism, African socialism, and the like – in a later chapter. Here I want only to enlarge a little on the philosophical answers. They may yet prove weightier than they seem to be at present. For a number of thinkers have begun to search for a social cement, if one may call it that, capable of giving the concept of African unity a strength derived from traditional custom and religion, both of which are powerful because effective and venerable factors in African social thought: in the thought, that is, of many Africans in many countries about the standards by which they have lived in the pre-colonial past and by which they ought to live in the post-colonial future.

We have already touched, in the final section of chapter two above, on some of the fundamental elements in this line of thought. Apart from being a natural reaction to the familiar colonial stereotype – that all in Africa was 'primitive, savage, and chaotic' before the coming of Europeans – this line of thought is also a product of Africa's having discovered itself in the past few years. The old colonial notion that 'Africans have no history worth the name' is now seen – and, by Africans, with an understandable exaltation – to be wide of the truth. But this new recognition of long and complex historical processes lying behind the materially simple fabric of African life has evoked (and partly been evoked by) a new interest in African thought. The best of modern European and North American anthropologists have altogether abandoned the old condescension: what they are now concerned with is to show why African society developed as it did, why it did not develop differently, and why, in general, its forms of development deserve study and respect.

Their work has begun to throw a vivid light into previously dark places. Reading modern accounts of African philosophy and religion, indeed, one gains the impression that in no other field had non-African misunderstanding and belittlement of Africa gone so far. There now appears a consensus of agreement among scholars who have lately worked in this field that African approaches to the basic problems of creation and survival are to be regarded as no less meaningful and effective than other pre-scientific explanations, whether religious or merely metaphysical. West African religion, for example, was long thought of as a blind and furious fear of images – 'fetishes' – whose unpredictable behaviour only confirmed the general chaos and insecurity of life. 'But why isolate West Africa from the rest of the world?' Parrinder asks. 'This has been one of the most harmful effects of speaking about "fetishism". For there is not a single religious

77

or magical practice in West Africa that cannot be paralleled in some other continent. Magical objects abound in Asia and in Europe, and for a scientific comparative study of religions it is quite useless to talk about "fetishism" any longer.'[61]

Briefly, the same approach now governs the analysis of Africa's philosophical systems. The pioneering work of men like Rattray, Griaule, Tempels, Evans-Pritchard, and Fortes has revealed that such systems have existed without any need for inverted commas or for pressing the evidence. But it has also revealed that these systems possess a close common relationship over a very wide region of the continent and a very wide spread of social situations and concepts. 'We have thought,' wrote Tempels in his justly famous book, *Bantu Philosophy*, 'that we were educating children, "grown-up children"; and that seemed easy enough. Now suddenly we understand that we are concerned with an adult humanity which is conscious of its own wisdom, moulded by its own universalist philosophy.'[62]

This is not the place to open an inquiry into what that philosophy may be. It required thirty days for Ogotommeli, sage of the Dogon of the Western Sudan, to explain his understanding of the Universe to Marcel Griaule; and Dogon philosophy is only one variant of many which reflect the basic ideas of dynamism, life-force, and *muntu* – mankind comprehending 'the dead, the living, and the yet unborn'. It would require many pages merely to summarize the general ideas whose poetic reflection is at least suggested in the following lines on the nature of death:

> The dead are not under the earth:
> they are in the fire that is dying,
> they are in the grasses that weep,
> they are in the whimpering rocks,
> they are in the forest, they are in the house,
> the dead are not dead ...

It is another question how far such explanations can survive the scientific education which is now becoming available to at least a minority of Africans; though it may be thought that they will now, perhaps in a humanist garb, acquire a fresh lease of life. What matters to us here is that the universalist concepts of African philosophy (the metaphysical integument, as it were, of what used to be called 'animism' or 'fetishism') are now

78

being interpreted, more and more, as the ideological foundations on which Africans may stand in claiming to possess a common culture of the general status and influence as other 'world systems' of belief – Christianity, Islam, Buddhism – uniting otherwise disunited peoples. Here, for example, is a current philosophical interpretation of the basis for African unity. It comes from a group of Ugandan intellectuals who have summarized what they believe to be fundamental African ideas in the word *Ntu-ism* – from *ntu*, generic Bantu root for man or mankind:

> To us what is important is not the way the imperialists have classified us, rather it is our common attitude towards life, culture, and heritage. In choosing the name *Ntu*, we have taken it to represent a philosophy that runs throughout Africa ... Most of the ideas which reflect the African way of life are embodied in the philosophy of *Ntu* ... We would like to divorce ourselves from the European method of demographic classification of Africans into Negroes, Bantu, Hamites, Nilotes, etc. As far as we are concerned, these divisions are of little significance, because they are not based on any deep and thorough analysis of African philosophy. ... [But] we do not intend to revive the past as it was. ... We want to integrate into modern life only what seems valuable from the past. Our goal is neither the traditional African nor the black European, but the modern African....'[63]

It will be observed that these Ugandans are using traditional ideas not as the ground-work for racialist obscurantism but as a means of preaching humanist unity.

Summing up, then, we may think that the slogan of the African Personality has a dual content. It emphasizes African particularity over against the rest of the world (and therefore of African equality with other major human groupings), but it also affirms a basic unity within the countless diversities of African life. Of course, a slogan of such varied and widely attractive nature can take several destinies – from a black racialist reaction to white racialism (as with the 'Moslems' in the United States) at one extreme, to an internationalism or supra-nationalism which is now, as many believe, an indispensable condition of African self-realization. And obviously the slogan is flourished by all sorts of eager folk who bother little about its inner implications. The fact remains, in any case, that propaganda for the projection of 'an African personality' has widely come to seem a valid means of asserting the full humanity of all peoples in Africa, no matter what their situation. This being so, the ideas behind it will undoubtedly exercise an influence on the future.

6 The Real Colonial Crisis

Such have been the general ideas, or the more important of them, with which Africans have sprung into their years of emancipation. But what, really, was the situation to which the ideas applied? There had been much dismantlement of traditional society; but this was not the only consequence of foreign rule. To many colonies Europe had brought much, material and mental, that was new. Some of the new intrusions cancelled each other curiously out: fewer people fell victim to disease, because modern medical techniques protected them, but more people suffered from malnutrition, because larger harvests failed to accompany larger populations. Yet, in the overall accounting, these intrusions, industrial, commercial, ideological – and the list is long and interesting – had combined into a process of dislocation and disruption that was unprecedented in history.

Before considering what became of the hopeful slogans of the nineteen-fifties, we must take another look at the real situation in which they were applied. That is the subject of this and the following chapter.

While it is no safer to generalize about Africa than about any other large and contradictory subject, the situation in most colonies on the eve of independence – and therefore in the early years of self-rule – can none the less be summarized in one short phrase: acute and worsening poverty.

This was not, of course, the intention of the colonial powers: it was the result of a failure (in the circumstances, an inevitable failure) to reorganize traditional life on a new basis. Even in such comparatively favoured colonies as the Gold Coast, whose farmers produced most of the world's cocoa, there were regions of increasing poverty. 'There can be no doubt,' according to Dr Margaret Field, 'that in spite of seasonal bursts of spending on luxuries, cocoa has lowered the basic standards of living and nutrition. It has diverted attention from subsistence farming: the habit of steady diligence has declined. . . .'[64]

Some of the general grounds for believing that most economies in Africa were involved in acute and worsening poverty have been noticed in an earlier chapter. The traditional subsistence economies of Africa had provided on the whole a sufficient diet for their populations, as may be seen from the historical fact that no major part of Africa ever appears to have suffered chronic famine in the past. By 1945, however, they were far gone in ruin. Devaluation of the rural economy, coupled with the migrant labour system and the enclosure of land by Europeans, had reached a point of continental crisis from which no colonial policy-maker could see a clear escape. Official records of the last colonial years are loud with lamentations of despair.

A full review of this culminating crisis in a system which had never achieved stability except in stagnation – and even then only between bouts of 'pacification' – would have to consider many factors. Not the least of these would be the impact of 'world terms-of-trade', which have regularly cancelled out higher African production (as well as loans and gifts from abroad) by raising the price of Africa's manufactured imports or lowering the price of her raw material exports. Moreover, the rate of impoverishment has greatly varied.

This rate of impoverishment has been greatest, it would seem, in territories of permanent white settlement, and smallest in some of the more fortunate West African countries. Yet even in Nigeria, where the subsistence economy has survived to some extent as a valid means of livelihood (married uneasily, here and there, with production for cash-markets), an official report of 1951 showed that 51 per cent of children in the Northern Region died before they were six, while 70 per cent of all children admitted to hospital in the Eastern Region were found to be suffering from malnutrition.[65] For the country as a whole more than 20 million people (perhaps half the population) were thought to be living on an everyday level of a very low order, with widespread hunger and disease. Yet this is still a long way from the catastrophe which had overtaken most of the rural African population of South Africa.

Within the last year or so the government of South Africa has moved towards the creation of semi-autonomous African state-lets, known as 'Bantustans'. In these, it is claimed, Africans will be able to develop in unhampered freedom 'along their own lines'. Leaving aside any other aspect, consider only the physical situation of these 'Bantustans'. They are, of course, the old Native Reserves under a new name – the ten or twelve per cent of the whole land surface of South Africa in which three or four million people are supposed to live and prosper. The greater part of these Reserves was in ruinous condition as much as thirty years ago.* In 1948, the year in which the Afrikaner Nationalists came to power, an assistant director of Native Agriculture observed of one of the more important of the Reserves, the Ciskei in the Eastern Cape, that 'over perhaps ten per cent of the total area, the incidence of soil erosion may be described as slight; over fifty per cent as bad; over the balance, as nothing less than terrifying'.[66] Writing at about the same time of the neighbouring and much larger Transkei – the first of the 'Bantustans' – two South African medical specialists, J. and T. Gillman, reported 'ample evidence that among a population malnourished for one or two generations, the adults already harbour such extensive lesions in many organs that chances of cure are at present remote. . . .'[67]

But what was true of the reserves in South Africa was also true, in more or less identical degree, of other reserves in colonies which practised the same system, such as Southern Rhodesia or Kenya, or those which practised a comparable system, such as Moçambique or Angola; although in all these cases it is difficult or impossible to find adequate statistical information, either because it was not collected or, if collected, not fully published. 'Throughout our inquiry,' noted the East Africa Royal Commission of 1955, 'we were impressed by the recurring evidence that particular areas were now carrying so large a population that agricultural production in them was being retarded, that the natural resources themselves were being destroyed, that families were unable to find access to new land, and that land which should have been lying fallow was being encroached upon. Such a situation . . . implies that there must either be a

* See page 39 above.

change in the use of land or a reduction in the number of people whom the land has to sustain.'[68]

That was one aspect of the matter. There were others. One of these was the colonial emphasis on production for export instead of for local food consumption. We have seen what this meant in the case of Algeria.* (The earlier switch from food to cotton production in semi-colonial Egypt had provided a perhaps still more shattering example of rural disaster.) In the Gold Coast, much wealth was earned from exporting cocoa. But there were dwindling crops in other agricultural sectors: even in 1961, Ghana still had to spend some £26 millions (mainly from cocoa assets) on the import of food alone. Other countries, lacking Ghana's comparative wealth, needed the food but could not or would not buy it. Much good land in Southern Rhodesia went into the production of tobacco, a crop from which Africans could gain nothing except wages at a rate unusually low even for the southern regions of the continent. The Belgian Congo offered similar examples: large quantities of African land and labour were taken out of local food production for the benefit of export crops. Portuguese colonial policy has enforced cotton cultivation over substantial areas of Angola and Moçambique. Some of the results were described by the Bishop of Beira in 1950:

Whoever has frequent contact with certain of the cotton zones [of northern Moçambique] has no difficulty in recognizing that the principal effort of the native ... is absorbed by the cotton, and that there remains not much time or effort to grow food which is needed by him and by others. I know a region which used to be a granary for lands afflicted with hunger. After the cotton campaign was begun there, the fertile fields ceased to supply food for the neighbouring populations and the people of the region itself also began to feel hunger. There belongs to my diocese a region in which for six months the black spectre of hunger reaped the lives of the inhabitants. ...[69]

None of this was denied by officials – or not, at any rate, in their moments of reflection. Many conscientious men of good will sought for solutions to a crisis whose existence all admitted. It is not a question, needless to say, of loading guilt on the shoulders of colonial administrators who were often, as individ-

* See page 39 above.

uals, admirable in their attempts to deal with a situation which was simply too much for them. But there is a great need to see this situation as it really was; and as, to a considerable extent, it still is.

Rural Africa was dying on its feet. But surely the compensation, the way out, lay in the new industries and economic options which colonial enterprise was bringing into the continent? Yet all these rested on African labour; and African labour, more often than not, was migrant labour. If ever there was an argument for the ultimate validity of Pan-African ideas, surely it lay here. Year after year, from one end of the continent to the other, countless hundreds and thousands of men could be found trudging on foot from territory to territory – unless their prospective employers, like the South African gold mines, had got the migrant system so well organized that they could provide lorries, trains, and even aeroplanes.

Borders and frontiers, closed or open, made no difference to this ceaseless movement of men in search of wages: the sheer need to earn money (initially to pay taxes, afterwards to ensure survival of their families) drove them across every obstacle. In an average year, for example, half the total force of able-bodied men in Basutoland is away working in South Africa. The proportion for Nyasaland has often been almost as high. Tanganyika attracts 40,000 migrants every year from Ruanda, Urundi, and Moçambique. In West Africa the plantation economy of the Ivory Coast rests on labour from neighbouring Upper Volta; an even larger number of peasants from Upper Volta goes annually to Ghana. A map of all these annual migrations, sketched across Africa, would show a cobweb of trodden paths.

This many-sided movement, repeated year by year, has had profound social consequences; and none of them can be said to have been good. One has been to hasten the decline of rural areas where over-population had not been a cause of poverty. Traditional disciplines have disappeared with this steady drain of the very individuals who would otherwise best exercise them. 'The young people go off to the towns, life dies out in villages which are sad and comfortless, without sufficient food, where forced labour services pile up without any hope of a man's seeing an end to them, where sickness is widespread without the European's fighting against it . . .': such was the conclusion of a by no

means radically minded Belgian observer in the Congo of 1946.[70]
It would be easy to lay other such testimony alongside his.
The 'economic options' of colonial enterprise proved powerless
to solve the rural crisis; on the contrary, they only deepened it.

Then perhaps the way out, the one escape from the crisis, lay
in the new African towns and cities? Steady urban employment
for a living wage was undoubtedly the right solution; but urban
employment was for the most part neither steady nor exchanged
for a living wage. The round figures, true enough, are impressive.
It may be that as many as nine or ten million Africans south of
the Sahara, and some three millions to the north of it, were
classifiable as wage-earning workers by the last years of the
colonial period: perhaps six to eight per cent of the total population, compared with a very much smaller fraction ten or
twenty years earlier. But the round figures tell little of the story.

To begin with, a considerable proportion of these workers
were migrants 'on contract'. They were men who came to work
in mines and plantations for their keep as well as for a small wage
of which they could take home part (often a very small part) to
their families at the end of periods of six or twelve months, or
even longer. At best, these men could be said to be subsidizing
rural poverty; at worst, they were merely surviving as individuals. Only rarely could they become components in a new industrial system that was integrated with the needs and capacities of
their own people. Generally their labour was little more than a
means of saving the colonial economic balance from complete
upset. Thus Algerian migrant labour in France was the mere
counterpart of rural poverty at home – a poverty which resulted
from the production of wine for export, low wages and low
peasant productivity, coupled with the life-saving mechanism of
modern medicine. The same is true of many other African countries. Such primitive economic systems had no inherent expansive capabilities: they merely helped to tide men over from one
lean year to the next.

There were other deplorable effects. The colonial records are
full of complaints against a migrant-labour system which could
offer men neither the stability of village life nor access to a new
life in the towns. The case of South Africa is once again flagrant

but only, one suspects, because so much more is known about South Africa than about other countries where conditions have been much the same. Here the truth was exposed in a memorable statement by a South African Secretary for Health fifteen years ago. Dr Gale pointed out that the 300,000 or so workers recruited for the South African mines were fit when they reached Johannesburg, since 'the mines recruit only physically fit persons'. The mine medical services exercised (and the position is no different today) great care in examining their recruits for tuberculosis. They treated incipient cases, but they turned away those over whom the disease had gained an evident hold.

'Sample surveys here and there,' Dr Gale reported, 'suggest that some seventy-five per cent of those who leave the mines with incipient T.B. are dead within two years ... [but] in the interval they have spread infection' in their villages. Venereal disease, carried initially by prostitutes who attracted the returning labourer after his period of bachelor barrack-life in the mining compounds, was another obvious menace. Even the labourer who contracts syphilis while working in the mines, according to Dr Gale's expert evidence, 'does not always get treatment that is adequate to protect him from long-term effects of the disease. The gross early manifestations of syphilis can easily be cleared up by a few injections, and the labourer rendered fit for work again. But unless treatment at weekly intervals is continued for twelve or twenty-four months the disease merely becomes latent. There are no obvious manifestations ... [but] if infection is acquired at the age of 20 or 25, the breakdown comes at 35 or 40 in the prime of working life. Before this stage the sufferer has been rejected by the recruiting agents; and the medical services are powerless to help him. The mines had him when he was an asset. The rural area has him when he is a liability....'[71]

For industrial labour to offer any real alternative to a rural economy in crisis, moreover, it would be necessary for wage levels to permit the creation of an urban society in the full sense of the word: of one, that is, where men can live and prosper with their families, win a better standard of life, and embark upon the complex process of fitting themselves and their children for the modern world. Migrant labour has prevented this by preventing men from bringing their families to town. And even where migrant workers have been able to make this family transition, their wages have still been calculated, more often than not, on the needs of a single man.

This last point has been an important cause of *worsening* poverty. The general level of wages has been another. In very recent years, wages in secondary industry have considerably increased in some countries, notably South Africa, though this is not to say that they have kept up with the rising cost of living. But for the solid core of wage-earning workers, whether on white farms or mines, they have remained at a staggeringly low average. 'All in all, it is fair to say that the average African miner [in South African gold-mining] received in cash and in kind about 100s. a month in 1951, compared with 63s. a month in 1890.'[72] Given the fall in the purchasing power of the pound since 1890, it is obvious that the real wages earned by these hundreds of thousands of men fell steeply during the period. And this steep fall in wages, we may remark in passing, was accompanied by a corresponding reduction in the general working costs of the mining companies. 'In 1897, average working costs were 29s. 6d. per ton milled. Forty years later, in 1937, they were 18s. 11d.'[73] It is small wonder, then, that a radical African voice should complain in 1963 – after the Consolidated Gold Fields mining company in South Africa had announced a record annual profit of more than £7 millions – that 'the company is thriving upon cheap African labour inherent in the system of white domination in South Africa'.[74]

But South Africa, it may be objected, is a special case. Yet less so, apparently, than one may think. Like South Africa, Southern Rhodesia has operated a system of cheap migrant labour as the basis of its economy. Arguing that movement of African workers from country to town could not be stopped, Sir Godfrey Huggins (later Lord Malvern) pointed out in 1944 that 'the Europeans insist on this drift to the towns. They insist on having this native labour. ... We cannot exist for five minutes without the native today. He is absolutely essential to our wage structure if nothing else.'[75]

What was this structure? Sir Godfrey explained: 'If we went on a purely European basis with the present conditions of living and pay – I am not complaining about them but merely point-ing out a fact – the country would be down and out in five minutes.' Perhaps it was not surprising in these circumstances that a British sociologist, writing on industrial efficiency and the urban African in the Southern Rhodesia of 1953, should have discovered that 'the average urban African is unhealthy, badly housed, uneducated, and he lacks any security in town even if he happens to be born there'.[76]

There was clearly a great and urgent need for the benefits which, it was promised, the Federation of the two Rhodesias and Nyasaland would bring in its train. But what benefits in fact did that Federation, formed in 1953 and dissolved ten years later, actually bring? A United Nations investigation of 1958 gives one telling answer. According to its statistics, which are as good as any that can be found, the prospective Federation's crucial min-ing industry paid out £1,400,000 in African wages during 1945 and made gross profits, after royalty payments, of £5,500,000. In 1956, three years after Federation and a fairly sharp rise in the cost of living, the industry paid out £6,400,000 in African wages, but made gross profits of just over £80,000,000.[77] The change is interesting. In 1945 African mineworkers received wages equal to about 25 per cent of the gross profits: in 1956 their share had dropped to about 8 per cent. Federation was evidently rather more beneficial to mining shareholders than to the African miners themselves.

It would be easy, though tedious, to journey from territory to territory and expose much the same situation in all of them. The Belgian Congo in the years after the Second World War was generally supposed to be enjoying a boom. Judged by the value of its mineral and other exports, this was certainly the case. Yet a UNESCO report of 1956 could none the less find that children in Leopoldville, greatest of all the cities of the Congo, were in a desperate condition. 'On a conservative estimate, the proportion of undernourished children was about half.'

And what is one to say of British East Africa? There the Royal Commission of 1955 found that 'cash earnings per head of the African population amounted to only £3 3s. as compared with £8 8s. in the Belgian Congo. . . .' The Mombasa riots of 1939, the Commission recalled, had been 'mainly caused by bad housing'. A Nairobi official report of 1948 showed that *employed* workers were sleeping 'under the verandas in River Road, in noisome and dangerous shacks in the swamp, in buses parked by the roadside, and fourteen to the room in Pumwani, two to a bed and the rest on the floor'. Indeed, the position was noticeably growing worse. 'A study of official reports and the evidence of witnesses with knowledge of urban matters convinces us that conditions of life for the poorer Asian and the majority of Africans in the towns have been *deteriorating over a considerable period.*'[78]

Low wages, once again, were high on the list of causes.

The wages of the majority of African workers are too low to enable them to obtain accommodation which is adequate to any standard. . . . The high cost of accommodation relative to wages is, in itself, a cause of overcrowding, because accommodation is shared in order to lighten the cost. This, together with the high cost of food in towns, makes family life impossible for the majority.

And why were these wages so low? The Commission explained this too. Wage rates in the past had been set for migrant workers who came to town *without* their families. 'Their wages were calculated on the needs of a single man'; and yet, even though many men now had their families with them, 'this has remained the basis on which wages are paid until the present day'. These wages 'are insufficient, not only to feed, house, and clothe their families, but even for their own needs'. And the Royal Commission went on to quote the astonishing statement made by a Committee on African Wages in Kenya which had reported in 1954, that '*approximately one half of the urban workers in Private Industry, and approximately one quarter of those in the Public Services, are in receipt of wages insufficient to provide for their basic, essential needs of health, decency, and working efficiency.*'[79]

With such evidence – and large deposits of it exist in many and perhaps all colonial territories – it is hard to avoid the conclusion that the social and economic crisis of the forties and fifties must have erupted, if the colonial system had continued, into a *manifest* breakdown of the whole pattern of rule.

As it came about, the actual breakdown was largely concealed from the outside world. Colonial power withdrew before what seemed to be a purely political pressure, and the outside world tended accordingly to see the African drive for emancipation merely in political terms. It saw, more often than not, only the top seventh of the iceberg. But the bulk beneath the surface – the social and economic crisis – was none the less there. It was this that constituted the real colonial crisis, the heaviest burden left lying on the shoulders of Africa.

7 The Central Challenge

This, then, was not so much a political crisis, as a social and economic one.

At the beginning of October 1952 a conscientious Belgian missionary in the steamy scrub country of the Lower Congo was making his 'usual tour in order to enregister children for the regional schools'. He came to a place called Makakulu Tseke, where a school served about twenty-five villages. Here he expected to find 147 boys whom he had convoked, through messages to their parents, because they were old enough to go to primary school. 'I was not a little surprised,' he recalled afterwards, 'to discover that of these 147 boys, thirty-four were away from home in Leopoldville, nearly a quarter of them. And not one of these boys was old enough to pay tax' – and therefore to be under fiscal pressure to leave home and earn the cash wherewith to meet it.[80]

What became of these small boys? History does not relate. But the UNESCO survey of Leopoldville, three years later, found that most children there were well fed until they were two or three, but that after this age 'many children know hunger very early', while 'on a conservative estimate, the proportion of undernourished schoolchildren is about half'. What the survey called 'hunger-training' started at the age of six 'in most poorer families'.

The probability in 1952 was that few of the thirty-four boys who had run away from Makakulu Tseke to the big city had got themselves into school there. Most would have sought out an uncle or a cousin and found some kind of job to do. With or without 'hunger-training', they would have made ends meet. But the ways in which they would have done this were many and various; and not a few of them testified to social chaos.

One aspect of this chaos was juvenile crime. Here again the sociological records are remarkably consistent in their avowal of a breakdown in social life affecting most of the larger towns and cities. This breakdown flowed largely from a more or less complete disruption, under very adverse urban conditions, 'of the practice of joint responsibility exercised by the extended family for the upbringing of younger relations'.[81] Looking into the social situation at the leading Gold Coast port of Sekondi in 1948, Busia found the courts much exercised with youthful crime. But 'for every juvenile who is put before the Court, there are probably four who are not apprehended'.

What kind of crime? Petty theft, of course; but here in Sekondi prostitutes also played a part in corrupting the young. Thus Busia came into touch with 150 'pilot boys': 'virtual or potential delinquents fending for themselves by stealing, gambling, acting as guides to sight-seers, or directing European sailors and soldiers to prostitutes', many of them with no settled home but sleeping 'in market stalls, on lorries, or on verandas'. Their favourite bar, Busia records, was called the *Love All Canteen*; the sentiment intended was evidently not Christian.

Prostitution had become a major problem. Busia thought that here, once more, the main cause lay in a breakdown of the traditional order, above all of the closely adjusted network of responsibilities in African family life. There was evident an over-riding conflict of cultural values at many levels, but 'most prominently and most obviously of all in increased crime, prostitution, juvenile delinquency, unbridled acquisitiveness, bribery, and corruption ... the symptoms of a maladjusted society'.

Such maladjustment was revealed by every serious survey of African urban life during these pre-independence years. All the surveys traced the line of cleavage between the old order and the new confusion which represented – or might one day crystallize into – a new order; and their findings are strongly reminiscent of those much earlier reports which had revealed the misery of European cities in the early days of mass industrialism. They did for Africa, though at a more scientific level, what Engels had done for the British working class in his famous report of 1844,

or what Booth did later for the London poor. The total situations
– of utter upheaval and the crude destruction of old values by
new problems – were no doubt pretty much the same.

In the African townships of Brazzaville, for example,
Balandier found a notably low proportion of women to men.
'The result of this is that there is great competition for women,
and about sixty per cent of legal cases concern adultery, divorce,
the custody of children, claims for sexual services, and even
incest.'[82] Grévisse had much the same to say of Elizabethville.
Surveys made in South Africa and the Rhodesias reached conclusions that were little different. We have glanced at what the
Royal Commission thought about East African housing: in Dar-
es-Salaam, for example, it was calculated that 'the average
number of persons living in a room sixteen feet by twenty feet is
eight, and that in some rooms it is as much as twelve'. There
could be only one outcome:

the evils associated with the absence of family life – drunkenness,
prostitution, and venereal disease – are rife in the towns with large
African populations. A large proportion of the women who come to
towns to escape from customary marriages, earn their living by
prostitution or enter into irregular unions. ... The lack of family life
means the majority of children in the towns grow up with little
parental control.

There were protests and attempts at improvement. To see the
colonial period as one of simple disintegration would be to
travesty a highly complex process. There were many administrative efforts at tempering and reducing the misery of life. But
while it is true that something was done, here and there, to
alleviate individual distress, provide more housing, expand the
intake of primary schools, and supply the more obvious needs of
elementary welfare, it is also true that these efforts could never
be more than marginal, for the basic problem, the problem of
constructing a new social order, was beyond the capacity of the
system. The East Africa Royal Commission saw this very well,
though phrasing it rather differently.

In East Africa, the Commissioners pointed out, 'tribal units'
shaken by the dislocation of traditional life and the widening
vision of a modern kind of life, 'cannot revert to a past which
offered to their members no prospect of material advancement

nor . . . can they go forward, or even stand still, under their present customary, legal, and economic organization of land, labour, and capital. To go back to the subsistence economy of the past, or even to stand still in the dawn between the old institutions which are dying and the new which are struggling to be born, would be to court economic disaster.'[83]

Yet how to go forward? Government might do a great deal, but 'it must be realized that only the members of a society themselves can create a community. This will only come about when people have been drawn together into social groups by a common level of education and wealth, irrespective of divisions of tribe or race. . . .' Nothing worthwhile could be achieved 'unless all have equality of status as citizens'.[84] But equality of status meant equality of voting rights; and this in turn would mean an end to the colonial regime. All too clearly, 'creation of a community' would have to await the coming of independence.

It was at this point that the social and economic crisis spiralled into a political crisis as well. Very consciously in some cases, less so in others, the best of the nationalist leaders came to understand that the post-independence 'creation of a community' must depend not only on implanting a new social order in the towns, on resurrecting the villages and expanding the economy, but also and above all on the sure establishment of a new political order. And this last would have to have priority because only a new political order could provide the minimal conditions necessary for ensuring that the other objectives could be achieved. This is what Nkrumah meant when he proclaimed his well-known slogan: 'Seek first the political kingdom, and the rest shall be added unto you.' Others put it otherwise, but they all had the same thought in mind.

What was the extent of this political crisis? How far had the old political order gone to pieces? In parts of Africa, it seems, very far. A skilled observer in the rural Belgian Congo could decide as early as 1946 that 'nowhere any more, one can say, does the chief really administer his tribe; nowhere does the grouping remain intact', and that 'the ties which once united members of the same tribe, both to one another and to their common chief, are everywhere relaxed and often broken'.[85] This was an extreme case of the consequences of 'direct colonial rule', and perhaps it was an extreme judgement. The chaos that followed on Belgian withdrawal from the Congo in 1960 brought faithful evidence that tribal loyalties could still be crucial in deciding how men and women behaved. Yet even the stiff and costly 'tribal wars' in the Congo of 1960–1 were not, one suspects, quite what they seemed, but rather, perhaps, the desperate result of a seeking for some point of loyalty and cohesion when public security seemed altogether to have disappeared. This has probably been true even of Kenya, where 'tribalism' has sometimes appeared to have driven all before it.

'Don't be misled by all this talk of tribalism in Kenya,' an East African leader said to me at the end of 1962. 'It isn't the same as the old tribalism – the old system that really stood for a certain type of stability and even progress. This new tribalism is the consequence, quite a lot, of the parliamentary system you've imposed on Kenya. That system – what does it mean? It means jobs, handing out jobs to the clever few. But who are the clever few? Often enough they're bright boys on the make. So when they don't get what they want in Nairobi, they go back home and organize a gang of supporters – easy enough in rural Africa, you know – and they make a row, and you call it tribalism. But do you think the old chiefs would have stood for that kind of caper?'

Some Africans have clearly seen the hand of local Europeans in this Kenya 'tribalism', seeking to divide Kenya Africans so that European interests might be better protected.* And it was undoubtedly true that the constitutional plan which proposed in 1962 to 'balkanize' Kenya into a cluster of petty states owed much of its inspiration and argument to European politicians in Kenya. Something of the same kind seems to have happened in the Congo. Tshombe's party coalition in Katanga was called

* In a disturbing book about the Kenya Emergency (1953–60), for example, J. M. Kariuki, a Kikuyu 'detainee', admits the force of 'tribal fears' in Kenya but argues that the colonial government did much to aggravate these by its refusal to allow any countrywide, and therefore supra-tribal, political organization by Africans. The government likewise increased jealousy among African politicians 'by its refusal to recognize either that Kenyatta was the only possible generally acceptable leader, or if he was not, that nobody else could presume to usurp his place until he had rejected the offer and opportunity. So they delayed . . . the settlement of the relative power positions of the various politicians', and 'split the country into two groups.' J. M. Kariuki, 'Mau Mau' Detainee, Oxford, 1963, p. 166.

the Conakat. 'Who cemented this Union [Conakat]? We do not hesitate to say it: the European.' That was the judgement of a Belgian by no means unsympathetic to Tshombe and what he stood for.[86] Or 'take the case of the Baluba and the Lulua in Kasai', commented another observer. 'Their antagonism "flared", and was considerably more publicized than tribal fights normally are, when it was in the interests of Forminière [the Belgian diamond concern in Kasai] that these things should happen and be known to happen. When that ceased to be the case, the Lulua and the Baluba seemed to become gradually reconciled.'[87]

It is accordingly unwise to infer from such cases as the Congo and Kenya that 'tribalism' still counts for much with Africans – at least, when they are left to themselves. But even if it did count for much, the traditional political order could never be sub-tended into an efficient system of post-colonial rule. By 1953 – and I quote the Congo again because it was one of the few colonies with a good statistical service – nearly one quarter of all Africans were living *hors chefferie*, outside the areas of chiefly control, and the proportion was rising fast.

Much the same shift was taking place elsewhere. The chiefly order was doomed. Furthermore, people wanted to get into the modern world, and chiefly rule was identified precisely with the world of ignorance and subjection they were eager to quit. All too often chiefs had become mere stooges of the administration, and therefore opponents of all who wished to 'create a new community'; or else they had burgeoned under colonial benevolence (as in Northern Nigeria and Ruanda) into petty dictators whose authority far exceeded the norms of the pre-colonial past.* In any event the great majority of chiefs (though with reservations here and there) had come to stand squarely in the way of political change.

And again, whether this was really so or not, it was certainly believed to be so by a vast number of ordinary people, even in those regions of 'indirect rule' where traditional chiefs had cushioned the impact of colonial government. The case of the

* In an authoritative comment in his autobiography, *My Life* (1962), the Sardauna of Sokoto, Sir Ahmadu Bello, is emphatic that 'the old Emirates [of Northern Nigeria] were originally much more democratic than they were when the British left them'.

little East African country of Ruanda is instructive. At the end of 1959 the people forming the majority in Ruanda, the Hutu, took advantage of relaxed colonial authority to rise against their traditional overlords, the Tutsi. Constituting some four-fifths of the population, the Hutu considered that Tutsi rule had become oppressive and out-of-date. They desired to throw it off. And they were convinced that the Belgians, who had governed Ruanda as a mandated and afterwards trusteeship territory for forty years, had always sided with the Tutsi 'nobles' against themselves, the Hutu 'commoners'.

The Tutsi naturally denied this. Yet it would seem that the Hutu were largely in the right. As long ago as 1930 the Belgian Bishop of Ruanda, Monsignor Classe, speaking from a position of immense influence on government, had urged that 'the greatest disservice which the government could do to itself and to the state would be to eliminate the Tutsi caste. A revolution of that nature would lead the entire state directly into anarchy and to European-hating Communism. . . .'[88] This seems to have been the general Belgian point of view until the late fifties. By then, however, the Tutsi – representatives of the traditional ruling order – were regarded by the Hutu as part and parcel of the colonial regime: the one, they thought, should go with the other, and the sooner the better.

This kind of thing happened in other areas where chiefs retained some authority. Of course there were exceptions. Many chiefs in Yorubaland, for example, were active in the campaign for independence: to the point, indeed, that Western Nigeria today has made a consistent attempt to 'marry the old with the new' and 'make the chiefs feel they have a place in the new order'. With the creation of a House of Chiefs, there was an opportunity for these often able men to express their views, 'while ensuring that they will not be a stumbling block on the way of progress. At the local level the power to alienate land has been taken from the chiefs and brought back into the hands of the democratic councils. . . .'[89]

Some chiefs have made themselves the spearhead and symbol of political change, no matter at what cost to themselves. Best known among these, perhaps, is Chief Luthuli of the African National Congress of South Africa, who was awarded a Nobel

Peace Prize in 1962 after his leadership of the passive-resistance campaign against the aggressions of apartheid. What non-whites in South Africa have generally thought about Luthuli was probably well expressed in *Flash*, roneotyped news-sheet of the African National Congress and Natal Indian Congress, as long ago as 1952. 'They might dismiss our chief. They might take the chief to the utmost ends of the earth, but his destination remains unchanged in the hearts of his people, who are both the heirs and the stewards of his matchless dreams and his matchless deeds.'[90] High-flown words, no doubt; but their readers, given the odds, will scarcely have thought them overdone. And the great point about Luthuli was precisely that he had stepped out of the 'old order' and was leading boldly towards a new.

Now and then, of course, chiefs tried to have it both ways. They made their peace with the colonial power, but they saw that the alliance would not work. In 1945 the illiterate Balum Naba of the Moshi was put up by the French administration and his fellow-chiefs to oppose the 'nationalist firebrand', Félix Houphouët-Boigny, President of the Ivory Coast today. The Balum Naba failed, much to his own relief. For 'whenever he was able to free himself from [official] supervision, he told people – "Vote for my friend Houphouët. . . . What will I do in that Paris, with my forty-four wives and at my age? I can't speak a blasted word of French."'[91] And what indeed would he have done?

All these factors and others of the same sort have played their part in reshaping, promoting, or retarding the practical realization of key political ideas in the drive for independence. They have also, as we shall see later, given rise to new sets of ideas, doctrines, 'myths'; and their influence on all of these is not yet spent. Social and economic disintegration, political confusion: these were part of the challenge to 'new Africa'. But over and beyond them lay another aspect of the challenge. What sort of new Africa did people want? Did they know what they wanted?

These questions, too, have conditioned the thoughts and hopes of every African who has sought to play a leading part in the transition from colonial rule to independence. They were questions that were far from easily answered. Often enough they were fobbed off by sheer power of oratory, lost to mind in demagogic fireworks. They insistently returned. An outside view has sometimes portrayed the drama that was now beginning to develop as mere play between a handful of skilful or unscrupulous leaders and a vast following of 'simple village folk'. But this was seldom the case. Even when most cunning or least careful of the public weal, leaders have had to pay attention, even close attention, to what their followers expected.

In these preliminary years, the programmes were remarkably general. Just because the essence of African nationalism was a demand for equality and self-respect, they needed to be little else. 'Vote UNIP for an end to Federation,' ran one characteristic poster, on this occasion issued by the United National Independence Party of Northern Rhodesia in October 1962: 'Economic stability and prosperity for all. More schools and better education. Decent housing and better hospitals. Democracy and security for all. Independence.'

On the trade-union front – an active part of the independence campaign in many British and French colonies – the *Zimbabwe Labour News* of Southern Rhodesia appealed in September 1961 for 'one national wage' – irrespective, that is, of race – and reminded readers that 'we are moving into a new Zimbabwe in which labour cannot be content to deal only with wages, hours, and conditions of work, but must have an increasing voice in determination of economic policies'.

'Freedom is our birthright, self-government our heritage as sons and daughters of the free men and women who inherited Africa for the Africans ...' declared the Freedom Charter of PAFMECA (Pan-African Freedom Movement for East and Central Africa, later extended to include Southern Africa as well). Even so politically conscious a leader as Nkrumah had been content, in 1947, to summarize the aim of 'the national liberation movement in the African colonies' as being 'to win freedom and independence'. The early declarations all followed these simple lines.

Often they concealed more complex thoughts. Some leaders came to the movement in reaction against personal discrimination: what they wanted, at the back of their minds, was to create the kind of community which should palely mirror the advanced societies they knew, in particular France, Britain, and the United States, but with themselves in control. A few came to it from Marxism, either as more or less loyal exponents of the Soviet interpretation or as men who had quarrelled with the Communists and evolved, like the West Indian George Padmore, a variant of their own. There was the usual quota of careerists who said whatever seemed convenient. But the rank-and-file, in so far as one can safely generalize, only knew that they wanted a life that should be different and better than before.

The emphasis was on material change. More and bigger – and the flashier the better! All the same, as those tumultuous months and years rushed by, another note began to make itself heard: mostly, to begin with, from poets and writers whom nobody read, or nobody in Africa. Life in African cities began to seem ugly and unpleasant, and not only for reasons of poverty. Social values had turned into money-values; and it appeared that little else remained. 'Everything,' deplored a Congolese writer ten years ago, 'is dominated by money. . . .' Such was now the cost of getting married (thanks to the African custom of making a compensation payment or gift to the bride's parents) that to ask the hand of some girls in marriage was 'like asking for the daughter of a Maharajah'.[92]

Perhaps he was exaggerating. But he was not alone in his complaint. Whores and strong drink reeled across the scene. The 'old order', once it got to town, was liquidated in the literal sense of the word. Floods of booze poured in from every side. In 1951 French West Africa was importing fifteen times more alcoholic liquor than in 1938: alcohol accounted for 8 per cent of Ivory Coast imports in 1953 and 9·6 per cent of Dahomey's . . .;[93] and this was not exceptional.

There grew up a sentiment, at least among a minority, that political independence must prove a fraud if this was all that it could offer. 'Popular morality is now a wasteland, littered with the debris of broken convictions. Concepts such as honour, or even honesty, have an old-fashioned sound; but nothing has taken their place.'[94] Those words were written of Britain in 1962; but they could as well, or rather better, have been used of Africa. Independence should offer guides through this social chaos, as well as voting rights and parliaments.

Out of revulsion from this 'European civilization in Africa' there also developed a feeling that Africa might do well to search her own past for guides. The edge of that particular feeling emerges, for example, in Senghor's bitter comparison of Manhattan with Harlem (page 72 above). Here is another tributary influence to the general theme of the African Personality. Old Africa had not been driven mad by money: maybe a new Africa could show the way to sanity?

Thoughts along these lines, one must add, made little sound in the general cacophony of getting and spending. They were difficult to hear, and even when heard, they were often expressed in a style of verbal flap-doodle, not to say downright nonsense, that failed to impress. One cannot help sympathizing with the African writer who cried out, after attending yet another conference on 'African values', that he was tired of hearing about 'African this and African that', and couldn't they just discuss culture? Paintings in the central office of the Ghana Convention People's Party show how Africans invented a good many branches of modern science; while a 'historical pamphlet' reaching me the other day proclaims that practically all the great men of history, in Africa or anywhere else, were in fact Negroes.

These more or less neurotic or romantic exaggerations should not be allowed to obscure the serious reassessment of 'European values' that was taking place. On the political front this began to emerge in about 1961 with statements on 'African socialism', turned as these mainly were against the bland Western assumption that if 'free enterprise' was good enough for Europe and America, it must necessarily be good enough for Africa as well.

That we want to banish poverty is one thing [a well-known African leader wrote to me not long ago]. The setting up, as a social aim, of the creation of unlimited wealth may be quite another. If we accept *that* as our whole aim it can quite easily lead us to a distortion of human values. For isn't it just this worship of wealth, with its concomitant distortion of values, which – in some societies – has led the masses to esteem the wealthy striptease artiste, or the adolescent 'rock' singer, above the painter or the musician? Once a society makes the creation of wealth a matter of prestige, it's difficult to persuade individuals not to adopt the same outlook.

By the end of the 1950s, a good many thoughtful folk were looking at the 'free enterprise phenomena' then developing at a tremendous speed in African towns and cities, and not liking them at all. It may be doubtful if many had read Tawney's *Acquisitive Society*: their conclusions, in a general way, were remarkably the same. President Nyerere of Tanganyika, who almost certainly has read Tawney, puts them in this way:

> In an acquisitive society, wealth tends to corrupt those who possess it. It tends to breed in them a desire to live more comfortably than their fellows, to dress better, and in every way to outdo them. They begin to feel they must climb as far above their neighbours as they can. The visible contrast between their own comfort and the comparative discomfort of the rest of society becomes almost essential to the enjoyment of their wealth, and this sets off the spiral of personal competition – which is then anti-social.

No doubt allowing himself a little romantic licence, he goes on to argue that this reckless hunt for privilege is utterly incompatible with the traditional ethos of African life.

> When a society is so organized that it cares about its individuals, then, provided he is willing to work, no individual within that society should worry about what will happen to him tomorrow if he does not hoard wealth today. Society itself should look after him, or his widow or his orphans. This is exactly what traditional African society succeeded in doing. Both the 'rich' and the 'poor' individual were completely secure in African society. ... Nobody starved, either of food or of human dignity, because he lacked personal wealth: he could depend on the wealth possessed by the community of which he was a member.

This line of thought was accompanied by another. The old ideal of African nationalists had simply been to 'join the family of independent nations'. But now it became clear that the 'family' was profoundly divided within itself. Even before the bonds of 'trusteeship' were loosened from them, Africans found their masters and governors eagerly urging them to throw in their lot, once and for all, with the 'West' against the 'East'. No doubt if there had been any strong Communist parties in Africa outside the Arab states of the north, these would have weighed in with a directly opposite appeal. As it was, many nationalist leaders and parties found themselves placed before an alternative they were increasingly reluctant to take. Was their new-found independence to be submerged, even before it had really broken the surface, within another kind of alliance among the wealthy Powers? If so, what kind of independence could this mean for Africa? They increasingly rejected the alternative. Following India's lead, they declared for 'neutralism and non-alignment'.

This was at first denounced by the 'West' as undercover communism, and by the 'East' as surrender to the ex-colonial Powers. Both underestimated the drive and purpose that lay behind the independence movements, which wanted – with growing self-awareness – to find their own way forward.

Thus it came about that the central challenge of transition was posed repeatedly in terms of *choice*. Whichever way they looked, leaders at all levels were faced with an imperative need to choose. They were not required, as had been promised, merely to set forth upon 'a broad clear road to freedom' made duly smooth and ready by a far-seeing and fatherly trustee. On the contrary, they were confronted with unprecedented mess and muddle – social, economic, and political. To make any sense of this they would have to select their own line of march.

Very few were ready for this. Very few had any doctrine or ideology of government that was more than a hotch-potch of colonial practice, coupled now with a reinforced pressure of personal ambition and traditional custom.

But there was also the pressure of mass demands for the better life that independence had seemed to proffer. And this pressure was no less imperative. Under its influence, new solutions began to appear. They appeared sooner than had seemed likely or even possible. These are the solutions in which, with widely varying results, the vague aspirations of the African awakening have now begun to take shape.

8 Towards a New Society?

The rise of popular nationalism was accordingly not just a political reaction to colonial rule. It was also a movement of social regeneration.

In this respect, of course, it was like other popular movements in other lands. Whole populations, previously quite apathetic to politics, were suddenly found to be imbued with startling new ideas. But the colonial governors, few of whom had ever known any personal political activity or thought about politics in more than the administrative sense – as a game of hide-and-seek between 'policemen and agitators' – could seldom understand or believe this new phenomenon. They therefore concluded, and with a dismal uniformity of conviction, that all demands were the work of irresponsible malcontents or sinister agents (probably Communist). To put it mildly, this led to misunderstandings.

Early in 1952 I happened to be travelling through what was then the colonial federation of French West Africa. This was at a time when the Union Française, liberal-minded legatee of the old French Empire, had lost its initially hopeful shine; and administration was retiring once more into an imperial frame of mind. Hundreds of 'agitators' were in jail. Violent clashes in the Ivory Coast a year earlier had cost the lives of fifty-three Africans even by official figures. The atmosphere was tense, not to say hostile. It became a rather delicate business, even a matter of gentle intrigue, for a foreigner to meet African leaders.

From Dakar on the far west coast I went up to Bamako – staid old market city on the Middle Niger that was then the capital of the Soudan Territory and is now the capital of the Mali Republic – with the object of meeting two prominent nationalists, Abdoulaye Diallou and the late Mamadou Konaté. I had taken care to provide myself with a suitable note of introduction. The problem was how to present it. Bamako had no telephone directory, or none that covered the African suburbs. Whom should one sensibly ask for directions? I sat in a hot little bar and found no answer. At last, prodded by a growing sense of futility, I took the easiest course and asked the French-speaking African barman.

The consequences of doing this were instructive.

'Look here, I've got to find Abdoulaye Diallou.'

'Ah . . .' A pause. A slight sense of pain in a comfortable face. The withdrawal of a personality, something like a light being switched off. I recognized the situation from experience in occupied Europe during the war, and hastened to produce my note of introduction.

The barman took this without pleasure and read it carefully. I began thinking I had made a fool of myself: weren't all barmen said to be honorary policemen? Holding my note, he stepped into the road. I wondered where he was going. He wasn't going anywhere. He simply stood in the road until the first cyclist appeared. This was a ragged youth on an old bicycle. The barman stopped this youth as though he had known him for years, gave him my note and some vigorous instructions, and returned to the bar, waving a signal that I should wait.

I waited. Half an hour went by. Then another. I was getting restive, but the barman merely shook his head. Eventually the youth came back, pushing his bicycle because he was accompanied by two fellow-countrymen on foot. One of these came up to me. 'Well, if you don't mind walking, we can take you to Diallou.' Which they did. Had the barman known the ragged youth on the bicycle beforehand? No, but the youth was riding a bicycle, and could take a message.

The passage of politics from a handful of educated men to a mass of ordinary people was never more fully revealed to me than during that stay in Bamako. The lessons continued. A day or so later I was sitting with Mamadou Konaté in his big old-fashioned house of clay in the *cité indigène*. He was surrounded by friends and adherents; all the same, he seemed unwilling to say very much. I was puzzled to know why. Upon returning to my hotel, a clerk at the desk gave me a folded sheet of paper. 'I think it's from the police,' he said. It was. Would I present myself to the Chef de la Sûreté? 'I expect it's only for your passport,' said the clerk, trying to look as if he meant it.

The head of security was politeness itself. A sturdy man somewhat given to corpulence, he took after Mr Dombey's Major Bagstock, and had the same quality of sudden fervour and the same suggestion of being on the point of bursting into flame. The upshot of what he wanted to say was that he understood all about my talk with Mamadou Konaté and that what *I* should now understand – for my own good, for everyone's – was that men like Konaté were either of no importance, none at all, or else were 'absolutely on our side'.

Mamadou Konaté became one of the founders of the Republic of Mali, and Bamako today has a handsome avenue named after him. The head of security had misunderstood the political realities under his nose, though of course he was not alone in that respect. Energetic heads of security all over Africa were making the same mistake. But a further lesson of this little story emerged the following day. Two or three friends came to see me off at the airways office.

'There were spies at that meeting of mine with Konaté.' It was, I thought, useful information. They ought to know.

They only laughed. 'It's regrettable,' they agreed, after listening to my tale, 'but we knew. Two men along the wall with the others outside the big window.'

'You might have warned me.'

'Oh, we told Konaté. And if we'd told you as well those spies might have guessed we had our eye on them. Then the police might have guessed that too, and sacked them. Very bad, you see, because it takes time to discover exactly who the spies are.'

Politics in Africa during the 1950s, in short, ceased to be a minority affair and became a mass movement, passionate and popular, within boundaries shifted far beyond the narrow limits of the past.

This was the positive side to the disintegration of colonial life. And this, one may perhaps repeat, was the over-riding pressure on political leaders who might otherwise have been well enough content to let things slide, and merely feed themselves fat on the fruits of office. Not a few leaders have done just that. Some are still doing it. More than one well-known figure has arduously spent his time, these last few years, not in working for his country, but in finding ways to convert public revenue into personal income.

Yet nest-featherers, though not exactly rare, are none the less no longer characteristic of what really counts in the political life of the more important and dynamic independent countries. In these, even while such scandals here and there persist and flourish, the pressures of public opinion for a new society, together with the manifest incapacity of the existing order, have begun to make for constructive change. The early slogans have begun to acquire practical shape.

Among these are policies which may be grouped under the heading of the 'one-party state', specifically defined, more often than not, as socialist in trend.

The One-Party State

Not all one-party states are heading, or intending to head, in a socialist direction. The True Whig Party has ruled Liberia, with one or two brief intervals, for nearly a hundred years; but not with any socialist intentions. The political structure of another one-party state (in effect if not in theory), the Ivory Coast, has often been said to reflect little more than the interests of a ruling African plantocracy whose ideas, once again, are far removed from socialism. For even if it is true, as a sympathetic French observer has written, that although 'venerated and protected by his Negro and white entourage as though he were a Living Buddha, the object of an adulation which he has never sought but which is lavished on him both by official and un-official people, President Houphouët-Boigny has not acted either as a dictator or a monarch',[95] the fact remains that nothing of any importance can be done in the Ivory Coast without Houphouët's initiative or consent; and 'H.-B.' is certainly no socialist. There are other examples of the same kind: in August 1963 President Youlou of Congo (Brazzaville) provoked riots by his decision to form a one-party state. This decision had nothing to do with socialism, but much to do with a wish to guarantee Youlou's personal power.

Those who have elaborated a theory or systematic defence of the one-party state in African terms, however, are all men and women who look to it as the crucial and appropriate instrument for creating a new form of *egalitarian* society. Their starting-point has been well described by Miss Margery Perham, though with a different context in mind. 'The first need for Africans [upon becoming independent],' she has said, has been 'to re-create for themselves the unity and order imposed by external authority and now suddenly removed.'[96] The first need, in short, has been to solve the central – and difficult – 'problem of power'.

In British colonies, and to some extent in French, the 'evacuating authority' left not a void but a more or less carefully articulated pattern of parliamentary rule based on European examples. There would be, ideally, a governing party and an opposition; or, with various forms of Proportional Representation on metropolitan French models, a governing coalition and a cluster of 'outs' who would form an opposition.

Now this arrangement presupposed many conditions which were in fact not present, or, if present, not significant. Above all, it presupposed a stratification of society along clearly under-stood lines of opposing interest – class interest – such as barely existed in any African country but Egypt. Potentially, there might be a peasant class and a working class and a bourgeois class; but the operative word was 'potentially'. Where class divisions did seem sufficiently marked to be recognizable, as in South Africa, they proved on closer inquiry not to be class divisions so much as race divisions. Thus the white miner in South Africa belongs to the ruling group as much as the mine-owner does, at least so far as attitudes and loyalties are con-cerned: a situation that was crystallized long ago in that remark-able slogan of the Rand disturbances in 1913: Workers of the World, Unite for a White South Africa!

Some observers, especially Communist writers, have liked to detect a 'national bourgeoisie' in African countries, notably along the West Coast. But while it is true that the Ivory Coast, for example, has an indigenous plantocracy which is beginning to go into business, and while Nigeria and Ghana, among others, have many enterprising traders and even a few bankers, these people neither behave as an investing class nor, as yet, consider themselves to be one. They do not have 'class coherence' of the kind with which we are familiar in Europe. They are simply men and women whose position tends in that direction.

This being so, there is no basis for the parliamentary democracy along Westminster lines which has always rested, and no doubt must always rest, on clearly defined conflicts of 'class interest'. Julius Nyerere has explained this from an African standpoint. He writes:

The European and American parties came into being as the result of existing social and economic divisions – the second party [that is, the Opposition] being formed to challenge the monopoly of political power by some aristocratic or capitalist group. Our own parties had a very different origin.

They were not formed to challenge any ruling group of our own people; they were formed to challenge the *foreigners* who ruled over us. They were not, therefore, political 'parties' – i.e. factions – but nationalist movements. And from the outset they represented the interests and aspirations of the whole nation.

We in Tanganyika, for example, did not build TANU [Tanganyika African National Union, now the only party in the state] to oppose the Conservative Party of England, or to support the Labour Party. The divisions of English politics meant nothing to us. As far as we were concerned, they were all colonialists, and we built up TANU as a national movement to rid ourselves of their colonialism.[97]

When colonial power withdrew, there was accordingly no effective pattern of opposing interests which could offer the basis for a stable multi-party system. For 'now the colonialists have gone', Nyerere continues, 'there is no remaining division between "rulers" and "ruled"; no monopoly of political power by any sectional group, which could give rise to conflicting parties.' If this is the case, what interests can be served by parties severed from the nationalist movement? Nyerere's answer is characteristic of others. 'The only voices to be heard in "opposition" [today] are those of a few irresponsible individuals who exploit the very privileges of democracy – freedom of the press, freedom of association, freedom to criticize – in order to deflect the government from its responsibilities to the people by creating problems of law and order.'[98]

Why should this necessarily be so? Because, Nyerere replies, 'there can only be one reason for the formation of such parties [of opposition] in a country like ours – the desire to imitate the political structure of a totally dissimilar society. What is more, the desire to imitate where conditions are not suitable for imitation can easily lead us into trouble. To try and import the idea of a parliamentary opposition into Africa may very likely lead to violence – because the opposition parties will tend to be regarded as traitors by the majority of our people, or, at best, it will lead to the trivial manoeuvrings of "opposing" groups whose time is spent in the inflation of artificial differences into some semblance of reality "for the sake of preserving democracy". The latter alternative, I repeat, is an over-sophisticated pastime which we in Africa cannot afford to indulge in; our time is too short and there is too much serious work to be done.'[99]

Such views have been little affected, except in the way of irritation, by continuous European and American criticism that lack of an opposition must lead straight to personal or group dictatorship, with all the familiar (European) perversions of justice associated with it. African experience has so far found little indigenous ground for such criticism or its implications. South Africa, for example, has always enjoyed a multi-party system; so has Southern Rhodesia. But the situation of the vast majority of people under these multi-party regimes has been anything but 'democratic' – little different, indeed, from their situation in countries of frank dictatorship like Angola or Moçambique. If massive forced labour has disappeared in Rhodesia but not in Angola, it is because the British are a modern people who fully recognize the needs of industry, while the Portuguese are not. The question of 'local parliamentary system' appears beside the point.

Moreover, the nature of African traditional government – a theme of growing influence in these formative years – has seemed to throw convincing doubt on the relevance of European parliamentary models. Africa, it is claimed, knew democracy perfectly well in the past. The 'tribal system' had often provided for it. 'The Elders sit under a tree,' in Clutton-Brock's well-known definition, 'and talk until they agree. . . .' Those in the past who did not agree, and could not bear to continue under the rule of this or that community, either sought and secured destoolment of the elected chief, or else shouldered their spears and trekked to a new land.

Not only Africans have made this claim to pre-colonial democracy. 'It is rare,' Hailey observed in 1951, 'to find in British Colonial Africa any instance in which the indigenous form of rule previously in force could be described as autocratic, and there are not many cases' – the Zulus provide the classic exception here – 'in which it could be described in a strict sense as authoritarian.'[100] A Portuguese traveller among the Ovimbundu (Bailundu) of Angola put it rather differently in 1837, but with no less conviction. 'The government of Bailundu,' he found, 'is democratic. These heathen mix with the infamous humiliations of the orientals, the unbridled coarseness of the English people at election time in England. The kings defer to and flatter their counsellors: these are they who elevate a king to the throne and also cast him down.'[101]

Many others have reached the same conclusion. Rattray thought that the Ashanti constitution, when properly applied, was 'democratic to a degree'.[102] The notion that Britain brought democracy to West Africa, Dr Margaret Field believes, 'is quite erroneous. On the contrary, Britain did much to destroy the indigenous democracy. Neither is the idea of an opposition a new one. Alongside every chief [in Ashanti] was a *mankrado* or *krontinhene* of whom it was said, "every *mankrado* is opposed to the chief."'[103] This, of course, was 'institutional opposition': otherwise, after decisions by chiefs-in-council, popular opposition seems generally to have been regarded as treason.

The main point in this connexion is that African thinkers and politicians, reassessing their past, believe that it was often as effectively democratic as the best practices of modern Europe.[104] If there were exceptions in Africa, there were surely exceptions in Europe as well; and Europeans (with so many dictators in their recent past and even in their present) may prefer not to argue. Believing this, African leaders often urge that the solutions of the past, which had so often married traditional democracy to unicephalous rule, can point the way towards marrying modern democracy to a one-party state.

But having predicated the solution of the central problem of power by means of a 'democratically representative one-party state' – with the aim of gathering all constructive energies and initiatives into cooperation for the building of a new society – there still remained the urgent problem of choosing a model.

African Socialism

An American senator lately found the Minister of Finance of the Ivory Coast 'a great believer in the private enterprise system'.[105] The Minister, if speaking his mind, is not in a majority, however – at least as far as a general belief rather than mere lip-service may be concerned. Of the leaders of Africa today it can rather be said, rephrasing Harcourt while retaining a healthy dose of Harcourt's irony, that 'they are all socialists now'. In a later chapter we shall see how widely they vary in their socialism. Here I want to look at the pattern of thought which has led to this situation.

In those few countries where the ideas of socialism are taken seriously, this pattern has had two conditioning thoughts behind it. The first of these is that *political* independence can promote no real social advance – and therefore, given the pressures of mass demand for a different and better life, no stability – unless it is followed at once by a major effort at securing *social and economic* reconstruction: at solving, that is, what I have called the real colonial crisis. The second thought, linked to the first, has concerned the *kind* of reconstruction that can and should be attempted.

Between the proffered alternatives of capitalism or socialism, and against the foregoing background, the ideologists who have made the running have all opted for socialism. They have advanced a number of reasons for doing so. At the purely practical level they have pointed to the sorry fate of Latin America. More than a century has passed since the Spanish and Portuguese colonies beyond the Atlantic broke away from metropolitan rule. Almost all have remained part of what Senator Ellender calls 'the private enterprise system'. Yet almost all of them, today, also remain poverty-stricken, chaotic in social structure, bedevilled by oligarchical corruption and ridden by dictators. None of them has really escaped from colonial bondage. Not much thought has been required to prompt the view that newly independent countries in Africa may well follow the same disastrous trail – unless they can achieve, early in their independent life, a radical reorganization of the economic system they inherited from their rulers.

A European member of the Tanganyika legislative council put the case very clearly in 1960 when he wrote that 'Tanganyika is largely condemned', through its colonial heritage, 'to a plantation economy manned by labour at subsistence level', and pleaded for a genuine effort to change this basis of inevitable poverty.[106] Having the example of many years of Liberian stagnation before its eyes, West Africa had taken the point somewhat earlier. 'With the political power vested in the people,' according to Kwame Nkrumah's basic delineation of this argument in 1959, 'we are now in a position to launch an offensive against the remnants of economic imperialism which have entrenched themselves in our country over the past hundred years'; and he went on to define Ghana's second development plan as 'an expression of the will and determination of the people to break through the barriers of economic backwardness on the broadest possible front and to make possible a great increase in national productivity'. Three years later, these general ideas were being crystallized in terms of a specifically socialist programme.

For it proved that radical economic change – and nothing less was needed – could not be achieved through the efforts of private enterprise. There had been, true enough, a long history of capitalist venture by West Coast Africans. As early as 1880 Africanus Horton and others in the Gold Coast (Ghana today) had tried – and failed – to float a syndicate to mine gold.

'Inevitably, Africans found it more difficult [than Europeans] to raise capital; apart from a few prosperous traders and lawyers, the process of capital accumulation had barely begun, and the idea of investing it in business enterprise was totally new.'[107] A year earlier had also seen the floating of the West African Railroad, Tramways, and Canal Company, 'but the shareholders were not forthcoming'.

The failure continued. The years 1951–61 were something of a halcyon period for private enterprise in Ghana; but what came of them? Many individuals made money, heaps of money; few or none proved willing to put it into the kind of investment that is required to make capitalism 'work'. But how can you have capitalism without capitalists? 'You cannot mobilize capital from our traders and businessmen,' a Ghanaian leader, Kojo Botsio, commented when I raised this point with him in 1960,* 'they will not do it. We have in fact helped our Ghanaian businessmen over the past few years with loans for their capitalist development. Very large sums, too. And nearly all of it has been wasted.' Nkrumah drew the same conclusion in a key-note speech. If Ghana was really to go ahead, 'it can only be through cooperative and similar bodies, since experience has shown that private Ghanaian businessmen cannot or will not work on a sufficient scale to compete with overseas firms'.[108]

If this was so in Ghana, one of Africa's richer states, with sterling reserves of more than £200 millions on the day of independence, what could be the position in really impoverished countries like Tanganyika? When Tanganyika became independent in 1961 there were no African capitalists at all: there were a handful of European companies with oversea shareholders and a cluster of Asian traders, the first owing no final allegiance to the country and the second having no concept of developing capitalism in Tanganyika in anything but a primitive commercial sense.

To choose capitalism, then, appeared to mean one of two things: either a very long period of very slow development, the passage of enough time for a few to grow rich before 'passing on the benefits to others', or else (and perhaps in any case) an equally long period of close economic tutelage to the wealthy countries of the Western world – the very countries, for the most part, which had combined to produce the chaos of African life. Neither possibility seemed capable of offering any genuine hope of rapid economic expansion and social reorganization. This being so, the one or the other would very likely call for highly authoritarian forms of government capable of repressing the discontented, decapitating their leaders, and generally 'sitting on the safety-valve of social progress'. A democratic capitalism would be no more possible in Africa today than it had been in Europe a century ago. Indeed, the real danger to democracy would lie precisely in trying to stick to those very 'free enterprise'

* Mr Botsio afterwards became the Foreign Minister of Ghana.

patterns so eagerly sponsored by Western Europe and America.

By 1961, with such thoughts as these in mind, all those leaders whose governments were based on broad mass movements, as distinct from minority groups of one sort or another, had opted for the socialist alternative. Notable among these were the leaders of Ghana, Guinea, and Mali in West Africa, and of Tanganyika in East Africa (with those of North Africa offering some variants of their own).

In assessing their degree of conviction, and the form it took, one needs to look back a little. Many who had lived in Europe during the forties and early fifties had become strongly imbued with socialist ideas: as witness, for example, that section of the Pan-Africanist declaration of 1945 in which the delegates condemned 'the monopoly of capital and the rule of private wealth and industry for private profit alone', and welcomed 'economic democracy as the only real democracy'. And while the initial six-point programme of the Convention People's Party, formed by Nkrumah in 1949 to fight for Gold Coast independence, had contained no reference to socialism, the implications of the party constitution were a clear guide to the atmosphere of thought in which the programme was conceived. The CPP, it was laid down, should 'work with other nationalist, democratic, and socialist movements in Africa and other continents, with a view to abolishing imperialism, colonialism, racialism, tribalism, and all forms of national and racial oppression and economic inequality among nations, races, and peoples, and [should] support all action for World Peace'. The last point may seem anodyne today; in 1949, however, it was tantamount to a declaration of socialist opinion.[109]

Elsewhere the accent was clearer still. Small Marxist study groups came to life during 1943 in the French West African cities of Dakar, Conakry, Abidjan, Bamako, and Bobo-Dioulasso. They owed their inspiration and their lead to Communists, whether French or African, and introduced for the first time a persistently radical undertone into 'French West African' politics.[110] After 1945 the election of African deputies to the National Assembly in Paris brought close working cooperation between many of these, notably of the multi-colony Rassemblement Démocratique Africaine (RDA), and the deputies of the

French Communist Party, then a member of the coalition government in France. The RDA deputies affiliated themselves to the French Communist parliamentary group: they usually declared (I was then a resident correspondent of *The Times* in Paris) that they had done this because no other French party would really bother with them; but there is no doubt that several RDA leaders, including the afterwards very anti-Communist Houphouët-Boigny, were then powerfully impressed by the Marxist case in Europe.

Translated to Africa, though, Marxist thought must quickly have withered and died unless it had found receptive soil in the circumstances of colonial and post-colonial transition. As it is, socialist declarations in Africa have taken forms and modes that often make them, from a European standpoint, notably heterodox. Of these the most interesting may be gathered under the omnibus label of 'African Socialism', itself a political complex of no mean interest. Here also we link up, among other things, with that sense of repulsion from the 'money society' of towns and cities which had begun to flourish and fester during the last phase of the colonial period.

This can be most clearly seen in the writings of Julius Nyerere, perhaps the outstanding ideologist of 'African Socialism'. 'In traditional society,' he claims, 'everybody was a worker. There was no other way of earning a living for the community. Even the Elder, who appeared to be enjoying himself without doing any work and for whom everybody else appeared to be working, had, in fact, worked hard all his younger days. The wealth he now appeared to possess was not *his*, personally; it was only "his" as the Elder of the group which had produced it. He was its guardian. . . .

'One of the most socialistic achievements of our society was the sense of security it gave to its members, and the universal hospitality on which they could rely. But it is too often forgotten, nowadays, that the basis of this great socialistic achievement was this: that it was taken for granted that every member of society – barring only the children and the infirm – contributed his fair share towards the production of its wealth. ... Capitalistic exploitation was impossible. Loitering was an unthinkable disgrace.'[111] And he quotes a Swahili proverb which advises: 'Treat your guest as a guest for two days; on the third day give him a hoe.'*

Whether or not socialism may be regarded as 'an attitude of mind', in Nyerere's words, or rather as a structure of society based on the public ownership of the means of production, distribution, and exchange, there is no doubt that the African tradition is seen as holding within itself a main component of socialist development: *cooperative* production. Even under the colonial regime, limited forms of marketing cooperative had often proved remarkably successful (especially in Tanganyika); and sociologists may be right in finding here a logical outflow from traditional attitudes to economic life. If Israeli achievement has won recognition in some African countries, this has been mainly because of the cooperative side of Israeli organization, although Israel's intelligently tactful modes of capital investment in the rest of Africa have their influence.† In the thought of Nyerere and those who agree with him, furthermore, the notion of cooperation is bound up closely with family and kinship groupings. Nyerere writes:

The foundation, and the objective, of African Socialism is the Extended Family.‡ The true African Socialist does not look on one class of men as his brethren and another as his natural enemies. . . . He regards *all* men as his brethren – as members of his ever extending family. That is why the first article of TANU's creed is: 'Binadamu wote ni ndugu zangu, na Afrika ni moja.' If this had been originally put in English, it could have been: 'I believe in Human Brotherhood and the Unity of Africa.'

'Ujamaa', then, or 'Familyhood', describes our Socialism. It is

---

* Mgeni siku mbili; siku ya tatu mpe jembe.

† By mid-1963, 42 companies based on partnerships between Israeli and African public capital had been established. 'Instead of demanding control, or concessions for long periods, the Israelis almost invariably postulate as a condition of their participation that their shareholding *must* be minority. Contracts are limited to five years, at the end of which the local majority shareholders are given the option of buying the Israeli interest out . . . Companies jointly financed by Israeli and African public bodies have been operating in Ghana, Liberia, Nigeria, Sierra Leone, Ivory Coast, Dahomey, Niger, Upper Volta, Senegal, Tanganyika, and two or three other states. In Ghana, the Israeli shareholders in the "Black Star" Shipping Line and the Ghana National Construction Company have been bought out, though they have retained some of their Israeli experts . . .' – *Economist*, 24 August 1963.

‡ Anthropological term denoting a family which includes uncles, aunts, cousins, etc., to several degrees, as opposed to the 'nuclear family' of modern Europe.

opposed to Capitalism, which seeks to build a happy society on the basis of the exploitation of man by man; and it is equally opposed to doctrinaire socialism which seeks to build its happy society on a philosophy of inevitable conflict between man and man. . . .

Far up-country in Tanganyika, towards the piling hills of the north, I asked an administrative officer of Kondoa what he thought this African Socialism, this Ujamaa, really meant? We were passing through a village. He slowed the car to a stop. 'There,' he pointed: 'look at that. Over there – *that's* Ujamaa.' Men were rebuilding a house, a clay-and-corrugated peasant house of the interior. One of them explained: 'We're neighbours. We're doing it for that man there.' The man in question hobbled on crutches, a cripple with paralysed legs. The administrative officer, not without a touch of pride, remarked: 'Neighbourliness – that's what we have in Africa. That's Ujamaa.'

From this classically utopian and moralist interpretation of socialism, we pass through many variations to the more or less thorough-going economic reorganization of such countries as Ghana and Mali. All of them, perhaps needless to say, emphasize central planning. But this emphasis rests on a reiterated statement that 'political independence without economic freedom' – the words here being those of J. S. Kasambala, Tanganyika's Minister of Cooperative and Community Development – 'is but an empty shell'.[112]

Accompanying this thought, there goes another. If political independence can be worth little without social and economic reorganization – without the reshaping of society – then clearly this implies an entirely new kind of relationship with the former colonial powers. Even so conservative a 'socialist' as Mamadou Dia, ex-Premier of Senegal, could observe in 1960 that 'one cannot reasonably speak of a balance sheet' [of 'decolonization'] 'when one knows that political liberation does not confer economic liberation . . . [and] that aid from the West, instead of being real economic and technical assistance along the lines of mutual development, is often the result of a bargain wherein commercial preoccupations are mixed with strategic or even political calculations.'[113]

The thought behind such declarations – and there have been many such – is not that any African state can win unlimited 'economic freedom' and thereby 'go it alone', but that the necessary minimum of freedom *must* include a freedom of choice between systems. African states, it is argued, must move away from their colonial economic integration with the 'private enterprise' system of the West (without, of course, moving into the communist system of the East). Unless this happens, independent Africa can only follow Latin America into a new subjection.

Economic planning became the practical solution to this problem of 'escape'. Ideally, it was now seen as a transposition of the united nationalist movement from the political to the economic sphere: the newly-independent government, based on its own united popular movement, would move on from winning and exercising one kind of power to winning and exercising other and more potent kinds. A strong central authority would mould the scattered and chaotic fragments of the ex-colony's economy into a coherent and progressive whole, setting targets, finding resources, and realizing step by step all those objectives – schools, hospitals, higher living standards, and the rest – which mass opinion now undoubtedly demanded.

Planning became something of a panacea. Meanwhile, another doctrine was required in order to safeguard the right to plan – the right, as it was conceived, to *choose*.

Neutralism

Most independent African states have opted for neutralism. And this, in practice, has meant the refusal to enter any part of the Western defence system, notably as embodied in the North Atlantic Treaty Organization (NATO), or to make any corresponding commitment to the Communist bloc. 'Let us now look round and see what they are doing,' it was argued, 'and when we have seen all that for ourselves, and made up our own minds, then let us choose what we like – whether in one part of the world or the other – and apply it to our own problems.' The Nigerian Federal Prime Minister, Sir Abubakar Tafawa Balewa, is prominent among those who have repeatedly insisted that 'neutralism' does not necessarily mean neutrality, but 'freedom to choose'.

The argument, really, was self-evident. Genuine political

independence at this early stage – whatever might happen in the future – simply could not be made to walk in hand with anything but neutralism. Another Nigerian has explained why. 'Whatever may happen in the Pan-African field,' observed the Sardauna of Sokoto, Sir Ahmadu Bello, in 1962, 'I am convinced that our own sensible course is one of neutrality. You may ask how we can follow such a course and at the same time be the enthusiastic members of the Commonwealth that we are. The answer is that India manages to do it with considerable success, and so can we. We must not find ourselves in such a position in international affairs that we should feel morally bound to support some policy which does not win our whole-hearted or intellectual backing, or attract us by its obvious rightness.'

Did neutrality of this sort mean pacifism? Not at all. 'We must also make it clear that the word "neutrality" means avoiding commitments in the sense that we are using it. It does not have the special meaning, so often ascribed to it, of not taking part in hostilities. ... It would be incorrect to assume that, as we are neutral in peace, we should also be neutral in war. Similarly, it would also be unwise to think that we would automatically follow the Commonwealth into a war.'[114]

The Commonwealth, in fact, has offered what many Africans have found to be a conveniently loose framework for their entry into the world of independence, though many people in Britain do not seem to have appreciated the African good-will behind such a recognition. Nobody has been more savagely criticized in British newspapers than President Nkrumah of Ghana. Yet Nkrumah, comparing the Commonwealth favourably to the French Community, expressed in 1960 a sentiment from which he has not yet departed, that 'to us, the Commonwealth is a modern, flexible, and adaptable institution composed of sovereign, free, and completely independent nations'.[115] Could it be that what many British critics of Ghana have really regretted was Ghana's independence? Rightly or wrongly, a good many Africans think so.

Neutralism is thus a diplomatic device, primarily, for gaining time. As such, it has already brought some useful dividends in reducing the impact of the Cold War. I think of Bamako again. In 1960 I returned there after an absence of eight crowded years. This far-inland colony of France had meanwhile become the Republic of Mali. Given its geographical enclosure, one might have expected its degree of independence to stop a long way short of neutralism. On the contrary. Staying in the same hotel, I found, were delegates of economic-aid missions from the United States and the Soviet Union, Czechoslovakia, Yugoslavia, Ghana, and France. 'East' and 'West' occupied opposite sides of the hotel lounge, but they were all under the same African roof – not far from the Boulevard Konaté. Mali's ministers were employed during those busy days in the grateful task of deciding 'what the Americans can do for us and what the Russians, what the French and what the Czechs . . .' Here was neutralism in full array; and it really seemed a remarkable achievement.

Neutralism is obviously a flexible device which may grow or dwindle in importance. French atomic explosions in the Algerian Sahara, for example, have met with severe condemnation from all the important states of West Africa – and, with the Addis unity conference of 1963, from nearly all the states of Africa – while Nigeria even went so far in protest, at one point, as to sever diplomatic relations with France.

It soon became clear that there were significant differences in the degree of seriousness attached to neutralism as a state policy. Some governments have interpreted it merely as a means of squeezing money out of the East as well as the West. Others, pushing the concept a stage further, have seen it as the barrier to a new danger, which they have called Neo-Colonialism. This too has become a dominant theme, and seems likely to remain one.

Neo-Colonialism

Many definitions are to hand, the clearest coming from Kwame Nkrumah, who has called it 'the process of handing independence over to the African people with one hand, only to take it away with the other hand'. He has also defined it as 'clientèle sovereignty, or fake independence: namely, the practice of granting a sort of independence by the metropolitan power, with the concealed intention of making the liberated country a client-state and controlling it effectively by means other than political ones.'

When offering these definitions, Dr Nkrumah clearly had in

mind a number of the ex-French territories, such as Niger or the equatorial lands, whose freedom of action was – and still is – very small. But the concept has a wider application. 'The greatest danger at present facing Africa is neo-colonialism and its major instrument, balkanization. The latter term is particularly appropriate to describe the breaking up of Africa into small, weak states, since it arose from the action of the great powers when they divided up the European part of the old Turkish Empire, and created a number of dependent and competing states in the Balkan peninsula. The effect was to produce a political tinderbox which any spark could set alight.'[116] At the same time as arguing this, Nkrumah also told the National Assembly in Accra that 'regional groupings of any kind are a serious threat to the unity of Africa': they could only divide the continent to the benefit of the ex-colonial Powers.

The ideas of neo-colonialism have in any case added fresh arguments against 'trying to follow the capitalist example'. Given the general absence of an investing class, the Guinea leader Sékou Touré has argued, as well as the fact that foreign companies are primarily out for higher profits than they can earn at home (such being their *raison d'être*), the promotion of African independence within the capitalist system must result in surrendering the rate and course of growth to the decisive arbitration of the stronger partner.[117]

An English writer sympathetic to 'free enterprise' has recently developed the same argument. For an underdeveloped country to continue the unqualified encouragement of foreign private investment on terms the latter is willing to accept, he writes, 'would imply that, at the end of a decade, a very high proportion of the country's industry would be under the ultimate control of foreign firms ...'[118]: would reduce it, that is, to a semi-colonial posture. So the need to change the economic system – to displace the old hotch-potch of traditional-plus-colonial economics by a modern system capable of yielding large material progress – must inevitably clash with the very requirement of those firms which are supposed to be promoting development.

The issue has appeared, basically, as one of profitable investment. What responsible foreign businessman would recommend investment of his company's funds in an African (or any other) country unless a continued high yield in earnings seemed guaranteed?* But what responsible African government could *guarantee* that the interests of his country would remain compatible with continued high earnings by foreign capital?

From the African standpoint, this has not seemed an academic argument. Nationalists have watched foreign firms exporting very large profits year by year from Africa. Judged by what these men say and by what one believes they think, their main count against the colonial system has not been, as Hunter affirms, that 'colonial governments ... failed to develop their African territories'. It has been that colonial governments developed these territories for the benefit of Europeans and North Americans, not Africans. This point has been seldom understood abroad, perhaps because the large earnings of many great companies in Africa have generally been taken for granted, or else not noticed by the European or American public. Nearly £1,500 millions of British capital, for instance, are said to be invested in African countries, yielding an annual profit after local taxation of many millions of pounds, and repaying initial capital investment many times over. Another recent estimate showed that the average rate of profit on the £860 millions of British capital in South Africa amounts to about fifteen per cent, or almost £130 millions a year.[119]

The point is perhaps worth pursuing a little further, for it illuminates what sophisticated Africans usually mean by the dangers of neo-colonialism. Northern Rhodesia is a country desperately lacking in educational and other social services for Africans, the reason being, as hard-pressed administrators have repeatedly explained, that there is 'not enough money' to pay for them. Yet the rate of profits-export from the mines of Northern Rhodesia has been enormous for at least twenty years: in 1956, to take a by no means exceptional year, about £50 million in company and corporation profits left Northern Rhodesia for shareholders abroad. This is certainly 'development', but of a rather special kind.

One could illustrate the same high rate of profits-export from

* Very few, in fact, have: since 1945 the weight of oversea investment by British and other private investors has gone increasingly into the developed and not into the underdeveloped countries. See especially Michael Barratt Brown, *After Imperialism*, London, 1963.

most African territories which possess deposits of valuable minerals. An official Gold Coast report, though for restricted circulation, had this to say about the year 1949:

> Of the £6·4 million earned by the exports of gold, perhaps £3 million can be considered to have been transferred out of the country. ... Corresponding estimates for manganese place the funds remitted [abroad] at some £2 million out of a total export value of £4 million. No estimate can be given in the case of bauxite. The three estimates given [in the Report] appear to work out at *something in the region of half the export earnings* [my italics], and, bearing in mind the very tentative nature of these calculations, it seems reasonable to assume that this proportion is a fair estimate for the remittances abroad necessarily involved in the operation of the mining industry as a whole.[120]

So far as one can tell, the estimate is applicable to the whole continent.

Whatever might have happened in the past, this very high rate of profits-export could no longer be regarded as acceptable; and some efforts have accordingly been made to reduce the drain of wealth. Exponents of the neo-colonialist danger have argued that there could in any case be no sense in *extending* such obligations to export wealth. The need, on the contrary, was to cut them down. But in order to cut them down, one would have to command an adequate measure of economic freedom. More than that: any later attempt to refashion the economic system along non-private enterprise lines could only be hampered by the existence of powerful foreign shareholders whose interests might then suffer; and who could therefore be expected to react in their own defence.

This line of thought has been vigorously confirmed by foreign interests, which have issued many frank warnings of the 'investment boycott' that could follow any attempt to tamper with the rights of 'free enterprise' in the former colonies. 'A break-up of the [Central African] Federation into its constituent territories ...' thundered a semi-official pamphlet issued in 1962 by a British public relations firm in the employment of the Federal government, 'must have certain obvious economic consequences. More than fifty per cent of capital in the Federation is owned by non-residents. Even if more rigid controls than those now operating were enforced, the repatriation of investment is likely to be heavy and the re-investment of accruing funds greatly reduced. Discount houses, merchant banks, and a fairly advanced economic complex involving the Central Bank and commercial banks would need drastically to reorientate their activities in such circumstances. . . .'[121]

Such warnings have been many, and have been heeded. They have been widely taken to prove that neo-colonialism is no mere figment of a fevered political imagination, but a genuine threat to any real freedom of economic choice in ex-colonial countries. For if the constituent territories of the Central African Federation, for example, were to advance at the general rate of growth decided upon, ultimately, by foreign shareholders who owned 'more than fifty per cent of capital', then clearly independence could lead to nothing but a repetition of the past: in other words, to massive disillusionment. Either these shareholders would have to stomach a cut in their profits, or Central Africa would continue to exist without more than the sketchiest network of schools, hospitals, local industrial development, and the like.

Moreover, even if African governments were to rest content with a rate of investment controlled by the interests of foreign shareholders, what kind of investment could they expect? Here again the facts have appeared clear enough. Outside the territories of assumedly permanent white settlement, very little foreign investment has ever gone into genuine industrialization and agricultural development: an authoritative American survey of 1960, for example, showed that only about one-fiftieth of American private investment in Africa (outside South Africa) had gone into manufacturing industry, while as much as two-thirds had gone into mining.[122] Almost none at all had gone, or could ever be expected to go, into the primary modernization of social and public services. For what profits, after all, were to be made out of building schools?

Reflections such as these, more or less widely discussed, have projected on to the political scene what may be called 'the neo-colonialist stereotype' – the picture of a situation in which development by 'free enterprise' must involve a new form of indirect colonialism. This stereotype has been repeatedly stamped deeper by much that has been said and printed abroad. The enfolding within the West European Common Market of most of France's former colonies was generally greeted in West Germany as 'an opening of the doors of Africa to other nations'. There was to be 'equality of investment rights' between these African countries and Europe; but who could doubt that the equation would favour the stronger partner at the expense of the weaker? German private investors had long been busy on the scene. By the end of 1958 the Deutsche Bank had become involved in more than 100 companies in South, Central, and East Africa.[123] Yet these enterprises, it was duly noted, went hand in hand with support for regimes which had been anything but favourable to African progress. In 1959 the West German authorities made a substantial loan to the Belgian Congo government, then desperately trying to prolong its life;[124] while other reports spoke of the exports of West German armaments to the Portuguese in Angola.[125]

Controversial or not, the conclusions were uncomplimentary. Where foreign shareholders could rest on colonial or semi-colonial regimes, they would gladly do so; where they could not, they would try to slow up a rate of development which could become significantly higher than before only at the expense of foreign profits. Further, these attitudes would be transposed to the political scene in the form of pressure on African governments to preserve the *status quo*, reject 'rash experiments', and generally rest content with 'what they had got'.

Such conclusions have led to a heavy preference for government-to-government lending and investment. More and more clearly, African countries are now developing towards a pattern dominated by state capitalism. If Western governments were initially reluctant to lend money at less than five or six per cent, they have since done something to cut down their rates under pressure of Soviet lending at $2\frac{1}{2}$ per cent. African governments have lost their fear that measures unfavourable to free enterprise would bring a capital boycott in their train. In this connexion, too, neutralism proves its value. By 1962, indeed, Ghana had achieved the unforeseeable success of borrowing huge sums for primary industrial development from both the United States and the Soviet Union. This process of 'looking to both sides' has gone so far that even so partially independent an ex-colony as Niger has entered into cultural exchanges with Moscow. The bold have opened the way for the timid.

A New Model

Within the last two or three years, accordingly, a new model of what an independent African state should be like has begun to emerge. It is to be a state governed by a single party representing all or most sections of the population, politically united over and beyond the traditional boundaries of tribal or regional loyalty, equipped with rapidly expanding social services, and moving out of the colonial economic system into a national economic system based on a wide measure of cooperative effort and public ownership.

Extending the ideal, it is to be a state living in good relations with its neighbours, subscribing to efforts at African union by functional organization and coordination of foreign policy while staying clear of non-African entanglements, and willing to make its own identity subordinate to the greater claims of an all-African identity. Its peoples will look outward to the rest of Africa and the world rather than inward to their own traditional divisions and diversions.

'The time of small and jealous nationalism is past and done with,' declared Gabriel d'Arboussier in 1958 when president of the Grand Conseil of a French West Africa that was then on the eve of independence. 'African history has often been the history of large units. All the great African states of the past were large or very large, and included many peoples. This was true of Mali as of Songhay, or of others elsewhere on our continent. But what the organizers of those old feudal states did by conquest, we in our day will do by federalism and by free consent.'[126]

The new African states have not achieved this yet. But in two or three years they have none the less made some startling progress in that direction. If a good deal of politics in Africa today still sound balefully separatist and chauvinist, there is another and more influential side to the picture. The key slogans and signposts of emancipation continue to be couched in terms of an outward-looking humanism, not of a narrow and jealous nationalism: a fact that must surely count as one of the grand achievements of modern Africa. And if the realization of unity is so far, across two or three crowded years, much smaller than the hope of it, that seems no reason for disregarding the nature of the hope – nor the movement towards realizing it.

This progress may be seen at several points. Not a few outsiders had predicted, for example, that Uganda would fall apart with independence, and become the victim of its own 'tribal conflicts'. But what in fact has happened there? By mid-1963 the shrewd Milton Obote, prime minister of a government struggling hard against internal separatism, could reasonably claim a large and perhaps decisive measure of success. The Uganda People's Congress which he leads was already emerging as a dominant unifying force, and was making inroads even into Baganda separatism. More than that: Obote had carried the weight of opinion into initial if qualified support for federation with Kenya and Tanganyika.

African unity may be much less of a wish-dream than sceptics generally suggest. It may even be true today that a large majority of politically conscious Africans (not seldom in contrast with their leaders) already honour the cause of unity as the only one that can continue to lead them forward. This, admittedly, is a personal impression; but I have not yet found any evidence to make me seriously doubt it.

9 Stumbling Blocks

Yet models are no more than models, however well designed, and human nature is not always what it should be. Anyone who leafs through the files of the last few years will find many occasions for stumbling over the blocks to sweet reason with which much of Africa is now bestrewn.

'Twenty-nine Europeans, including women and children, were given an hour to leave a hotel in Tanganyika today because they showed discourtesy to the President of Guinea,' then visiting that country. They had actually 'remained seated when President Sékou Touré passed through the lounge'.[127] Perhaps they had failed even to *recognize* the President of Guinea.

Prickly reactions of this kind may not be important but they have their place in the record. President Touré's Minister of Finance kept me waiting for an hour and a half, last time I arranged to be received by him in Conakry, and then without apology gave me a grudging ten minutes of his time. Travellers in Africa have learned to know that nationalism in Africa, like nationalism anywhere else, often has its underworld of thin-skinned pride and suspicion: understandable and long provoked, perhaps, but no more hopeful or agreeable for that.

Reactions of this kind would matter little if they were not the reflection of a deeper trouble. Africa won its political independence in chaotic transition from the old subsistence economies of the past to egalitarian and industrial democracy on modern lines. Withdrawing in deep water, colonial Powers left behind them far greater problems than any they had ever proposed to solve. This is not to suggest, of course, that they would have done better to withdraw later, since there was never any sign that they would allow the real problems to be tackled on a realistic basis. Indeed, the main solutions they proposed (and to some extent promoted) are in themselves a large part of the trouble. For what the colonial Powers thought wise and necessary was the formation and promotion to power of 'leading élites' or 'middle classes' (those whom the French have so revealingly called *interlocuteurs valables* – 'negotiators worth talking to'): groups of men who would ensure that post-colonial government should be 'moderate and responsible' – should be, that is, a reflection of colonial government. And it is here, largely, that the seat of the trouble lies.

For it is a fact, by and large (and generalization, one may perhaps repeat, will always be unfair to someone), that such 'leading élites' and 'middle classes' have largely collapsed under the strain of political independence. Some have retired into profitable corruption, others into old-fashioned habits of colonial authoritarianism, still others into a more or less sterile defence of the *status quo*. For others, again, traditionalist separatism (we may call it, with reservations, tribalism) has become a major outlet for their energy. And given their often great authority among ordinary people, the example of these educated 'élites' and 'middle classes' has echoed down the ranks of African society with curious results.

'For too many African "élites",' a notably pro-African French economist, René Dumont, has lately written, 'independence has meant taking the place of the whites and enjoying the privileges, often exorbitant, hitherto accorded to "colonials". To high salaries there are now often added fine villas splendidly furnished, or even palaces for ministers, the whole of their upkeep being paid by the budget. ... To the Peugeot 403s there follow, after independence, the Chevrolets of Abidjan [capital of the Ivory Coast] and the Mercedes of Yaoundé [capital of the Kamerun Republic] – often renewed after six months, something that makes ordinary folk grind their teeth. ...'[128] But who in ex-British Africa could not quote similar examples?

'Independence isn't for us,' a peasant of the Kamerun countryside told Dumont in May 1961: 'it's for the people in the towns.'

All too often, pressure for 'Africanization' by 'élites and middle classes' has meant that qualified foreigners have simply been displaced by Africans on the make. It seems likely that this process reached its lowest point in the ex-Belgian Congo of 1963, where Congolese were often 'occupying salaries' instead of jobs, simply because they were incapable of doing the jobs for which their salaries were supposedly paid. Here again the examples are innumerable.

They are also understandable, even natural. The same thing has been common enough in Europe. With a total of seventeen university graduates at its disposal, the Congo government was in any case obliged to choose between continuing to employ Europeans – in the event, those very Belgians who had occupied the jobs before – or promoting men without proper qualifications. Moreover, the collapse in late 1960 of the Congo's only movement of nationalist enthusiasm and self-discipline – a disaster that was mainly the fault of the Belgians and their allies – also meant the collapse of nationalist morale. After that it became a question of *sauve qui peut*; and who can wonder at this?

Continued semi-colonial tutelage has had the same effect elsewhere. 'These countries,' Dumont remarks of some ex-French states, 'have not yet understood that they are poor, because it is still far too easy for them to sponge on us. Apart from supplying the great majority of their investments (eighty-six per cent in Upper Volta), we balance their budgets for them' with financial aid. And so a little country like Gabon, with fewer than half a million inhabitants, has a parliament with sixty-five deputies: a Gabon deputy sits for about 6,000 constituents, compared with a British Member of Parliament who has an average of about 56,000, and a French Deputy who has nearly twice that. Moreover, he gets a salary which is equivalent to about a third *more* than a British M.P.'s. 'As for the cost of the presidential and ministerial establishments, with all their more or less useless journeyings back and forth, it is probably higher, in proportion to the national income of Gabon, than the cost to France of the Court of Louis XVI in 1788. . . .'[129]

Wherever the political assumptions of the colonial period have prevailed, in short, government in Africa tends to mean government by an oligarchical élite whose members are sometimes bound together by traditional ties, but more often by a network of private interests and activities of the 'log-rolling' sort. The early years of Ghanaian independence saw some remarkable developments in this direction, a veritable efflorescence of luxury living on a scale never thought possible before. 'Come and have lunch with me,' said a leading nationalist in those years, and, when I did, showed me with pride a mansion which must have cost many thousands of pounds. Yet the nationalist in question had not been a wealthy man before. Since then, happily, things in Ghana have changed greatly for the better.

The Nigerian High Court has lately had a field-day in pursuing post-independence corruption and malversation. When the Western Region Marketing Board began amassing reserves (largely from cocoa and other farmers) for use against a rainy day, it inherited a previously collected 'pool' amounting to some £40 millions. This rose to £62 millions. But early in 1962 the Coker Commission of Inquiry into the affairs of the Board found that these resources were 'now entirely scattered and, in fact, completely dissipated'.[130] Much of the money had been properly spent on various types of national development; a significant part of it had not.

We did come across evidence of prudent and considered management and investment of public funds and we also came across evidence of reckless and indeed atrocious and criminal mismanagement and diversion of public funds. We did come across evidence regarding some bold and courageous civil servants who stuck to their guns with remarkable fortitude in the face of circumstances of a most trying order, and we also came across evidence regarding some dishonest and callous politicians who had mortgaged their consciences to dishonesty in all its manifestations and indeed demonstrated this appraisement in the way and manner in which they testified before us.[131]

But what Mr Justice Coker and his eminent colleagues of the Nigerian High Court discovered to be true in this case would also, as everyone knows though rather few care to admit, have been discovered to be true in many other cases in newly independent Africa – had they only been examined.

Early in 1963 a reporter from the Algerian weekly, *Révolution Africaine*, had lunch with President Touré of Guinea.

We were five or six at table. A member of the central political committee, some Guinean ambassadors, the Foreign Minister. ... The guests get ready to leave.

'You've a car to take you?' Sékou Touré asks his comrade of the central committee [of the ruling Democratic Party of Guinea].

'No, President.'

'It's true – you sold your car and put the money in the bank.'

'One can't hide anything from you, President.'

Commenting on this little exchange, the President goes on:

There's a thousand reasons for these frauds in the civil service. Our economic difficulties are among these reasons. There are people who haven't been able to keep up with the situation, people for whom independence has become an end and not a phase.

Political independence isn't enough. What we need is to forge our economic independence. Among our party members, there are those for whom independence was first and foremost a chance to take the place of the *colon*.

But the current party congress, the sixth, would

open the phase of revolution: the strengthening of political education, the establishment at all levels of practical collective duties, the extension of criticism and self-criticism, and, above all, the reinforcement of the control to be exercised by the rank-and-file on those in power.[132]

A little earlier than that, in a dawn broadcast that was to become famous, President Nkrumah of Ghana had condemned luxury living, fulminated against the personal dissipation of national wealth, and appealed for higher standards of morality. All too often, though, the 'dawn' is still for tomorrow. Here again, there are other exceptions. One of the first actions of Tanganyika's independent government was to cut the salary of senior ministers from £3,100 a year to £1,800, and one of the first really important decisions of Prime Minister (now President) Nyerere was to quit his post and concentrate on organizing the rank-and-file of the nationalist movement in Tanganyika, with the purpose of setting an example for all those 'cadres' who thought, or might be tempted to think, that independence should now reward them with a lavish hand.

'Tribalism' is another stumbling block. In May 1963 Kenya had its first election on a wide democratic suffrage. Facing the major challenges of self-rule, this small country of some eight million people – deep in economic stagnation, deprived of any

great mineral resources, burdened with heavy unemployment
and underemployment – was none the less required to support
the cost of 715 candidates for 151 seats in the two houses of the
central legislature, together with another 185 seats in *seven*
regional parliaments.

Kenya was thus to bear the expense not only of eight parliaments and governments, but also of eight police forces, eight sets
of frontier control, eight judiciaries and other public services,
not to mention an eight-fold inflation of patronage which all this
administration would, in the circumstances, inevitably mean. If
it is true of much of ex-French Africa, as Dumont tells us, that
administration is now its principal industry – civil-service salaries apparently exhaust sixty per cent of total budget receipts in
Dahomey – Kenya was surely in the fashion. A large part of its
annual revenue was going to be spent in the doubling and re-
doubling of jobs and responsibilities of an administrative and
'representational' order.

This retrograde 'balkanization' of Kenya – since modified
by the wise insistence of Kenya's new ministers – was not
without its European driving influence. But that is obviously not
the whole story. It was an African party, the Kenya African
Democratic Union, which was immediately responsible for this
result, while tribalism – this time without inverted commas –
also played a part. 'Here,' commented a conservative but
shrewd English observer, 'two principles have run up against
each other in a conflict fundamental to mankind from which his
whole history has grown – the principle of advance, risk,
change, individuality, and contest, and the principle of withdrawal, preservation, collectivity, and roots. Here is the conscious
straining against the unconscious, the male against the female,
the spear against the heart. Here – to put it in electoral terms –
the tribe, the ethnic family, is cast into conflict with the idea of
centralized Statehood. All Africa is engaged in it.'[133]

This may be anthropologically poetic rather than incisively
political. Yet even if European influences had not striven to
'divide and rule', tribalism would still have remained a factor in
the present African situation. More often than some Africans
care to admit, the coming of independence has meant a certain
failure of nerve, a tendency to retreat within traditional

enclosures, a search for new security inside an old armour of custom and belief.

Various reasons may be offered for this. One is a rekindled desire for ethnic identification after a long period of colonial anonymity. Another, undoubtedly, is the force of kinship or of 'local-ist' tradition. A third rests in the survival of chiefly authorities and systems whose sanctions have always had the compelling support of religion. When you believe that your king is also the earthly representative and spokesman of God, you may think twice before turning your back on him. In quite a few corners of the continent, the divine right of kings still has potent meaning in everyday life. The Kabaka of Buganda is head of his 'church' in a sense far more obvious and meaningful, for most of his subjects, than Queen Elizabeth II's headship of the Church of England can possibly seem to the vast majority of hers.

But the problem is more complicated than that. Popular respect for traditional hierarchies in Africa is something, or so it has appeared to me, that orthodox European opinion has generally put too high. Given a chance to say so, it would seem that most people would after all prefer to govern themselves in a new way. And it remains oddly true that in nearly all those countries where tribalism has become most potent in the last few years, the circumstances of 'decolonization' have weighed greatly in making it so.

The average educated African nationalist, if one may dare for a moment to try to summarize the views of so complex a 'person', will readily admit that a post-independence reaction towards 'balkanization' – towards the decentralization of authority – is at times unavoidable. Where strong states have survived from the pre-colonial past, even if in tutelary form, the influence of their rulers is bound to be profoundly important to a great many local folk. This we have seen in parts of Uganda and Nigeria, to mention only two examples. And the same is true, even if less emphatically so, in a number of countries where strong peoples were in more or less frequent conflict with each other during the nineteenth century: as, for example, in parts of Kenya. In cases such as these, tribalism remains a major problem, one that will not be overcome without effort and probably not without trouble.

But this heady residue of ancient loyalties has had the addition of outside influence. That is what makes its real political strength so hard to assess. Had the Belgians and their allies thrown their full weight consistently behind the concept of a strong central government in the Congo, would the tribal wars of 1960–2 have really happened? Or, if they had happened, would they have been so fierce? Had the Europeans of Kenya, with effective control of policy so long in their hands, steadily wished to have a strong African government in Nairobi, would the pre-independence constitution of 1962 have taken its form of extreme 'balkanization'? Subsequent developments, whether in Congo or Kenya, certainly prompt negative answers.

Kenya has many peoples. But Tanganyika has more. 'Yet here in Tanganyika,' runs the argument you will hear in that country, 'we have almost none of this "tribalism" of which you speak so much. You'll find northern men administering the south, and southern men administering the centre ...'

'But you were fortunate in being able to build a united national movement.'

'Very true, we were fortunate in that. But we were even more fortunate in not having a large European minority concentrated in the heart of our country, and given large powers by the British government for many years. That is what happened in Kenya, though. And if you look behind the scenes in Kenya, you will see that those Europeans have pushed for "tribalism" just as hard as they could. Why? But that's obvious.'

This has been, no doubt, an understandable reaction by European minorities threatened with loss of power and privilege. At another stage one may now see the same reaction in South Africa where the Afrikaner National Party has sought to take time by the forelock in creating 'Bantustans', little African state-lets based on regional or tribal loyalties which, it is hoped, will reduce the pressure of explosive nationalism.

French Africa has offered other examples. There the active survival of chiefly loyalties, tribal loyalties, was more difficult because the French had tended to administer more *directly* – through their own personnel or through nominated Africans – than the British. They had thus consistently devalued and even destroyed the old hierarchies. This, incidentally, was why the nationalist movement in Guinea, under Touré's lead, was able so easily to suppress the pro-French chiefs of the Fouta Djallon. The population of those hills was in no doubt that its chiefs had thrown in their lot with the French, and it quickly rallied to the democratically composed village-committees of the nationalist movement. And this was also why, a little later, the Union Soudanaise in the Soudan Territory (Mali today) was able to reach the same end with little more difficulty. The French had relied on chiefs as props of colonial rule; but the white ants of 'collaboration' had eaten them through.*

Even the contrary cases prove the rule. Although commanding a big parliamentary majority in the Niger Territory, the Sawaba (Freedom) Party led by Djibo Bakary was overthrown after its attempt to achieve independence in President de Gaulle's proffered referendum of 1958 (the referendum in which the nationalists of Guinea were successful); and this occurred precisely because the chiefs in Niger were still politically strong. But the chiefs were strong because the French had made and kept them so; and, in turn, it was because they relied so greatly on the French for the further protection of their privileges that these chiefs (like some others in West Africa) were opposed to national independence. With the chiefs' support France was able to regain control. Niger is politically an independent state today; but it would be absurd to suggest that it controls its own destiny in anything approaching the sense that neighbouring Nigeria does so.

Senegal is a more subtle case. Its long association with France makes this West African country somewhat eccentric to the 'French African' scene: its first deputy sat in the French Parliament as long ago as 1914, and many of its townsmen acquired French citizenship only two years later. Yet in a muted form Senegal has witnessed the same struggle between modern nationalism and traditional chiefdom – the latter taking here the special form of *grands marabouts*, local heads of powerful Islamic brotherhoods.

* This familiar and rather comfortable British view of French practice is not unchallenged in France. In a brilliant and witty counter-attack, Professor Hubert Deschamps of the Sorbonne has lately argued that French administrative practice, up to 1945, scarcely differed from that of the British 'except for being more easy-going and less well defined'. ('Et Maintenant, Lord Lugard?', *Africa*, October 1963, Lugard Lecture for 1963).

These often vigorous men have played, and still play, a crucial part in defending the general *status quo*; and they have invariably enjoyed important backing from the French. Even in 1961, at a time when the independent government of Senegal was preaching the virtues of African Socialism, the leader of the Muridite brotherhood could still forbid the establishment of rural primary schools and dispensaries, while conditions of work on the lands of the Muridite leaders could be likened by a careful French writer to 'near-slavery'.[134]

When Senegal and Soudan joined in the Federation of Mali, the disparity of aim and attitude between the two countries' respective leaders soon led to scission. Mali had overthrown its chiefs and was governed by a party with wide popular backing and a radically socialist doctrine: Senegal, for all the distinction and intelligence of its parliamentary leaders, was still in the grip of chiefs and religious hierarchies whose intentions were quite otherwise.

Morocco's recent history tells the same kind of story. There the French found it impossible to persuade Sultan Muhammad ben Youssef to denounce the rising party of Moroccan independence, the Istiqlal. Like his forbears, the Sultan looked back upon a long and sovereign past. When the French banned the Istiqlal it was the Sultan who, at least in a symbolic sense, took its place. So they exiled him to Corsica and then to Madagascar, and installed a puppet whose name was ben Arafa. That was in 1953. It proved the beginning of the end for French rule. Far from cowed into submission, the traditional followers of Sultan Muhammad swung into line with the nationalists; armed resistance began before the end of the year.

Reacting to this along familiar lines, the French strove to bolster their power by finding other rulers who would play the tribal card. They turned to the Berber chiefs of the Atlas. Prominent among these was el Glaoui, the 'Pasha of Marrakesh'. The Glaoui and his henchmen were painted by the French as stern traditionalists who longed to be free of the 'Arab yoke', and whose people burned with loyalty to Berber tribalism. But the facts proved rather different. At the end of 1955 the puppet ben Arafa, having spent eighteen months in his Rabat palace without daring to set foot beyond the gate, fled to Tangier. The French bowed before the rising storm and brought back Sultan Muhammad. And the Glaoui? No resistance to Muhammad or the Istiqlal came from that 'man of brothels', as one of the greatest living French Arabists once named him to me. And Berber tribalism? Its burning ardour, if it had ever had any in recent years, vanished with him.

Colonial rule was here defeated by a traditional structure which had remained loyal to its history. But just because this traditional structure was alive and meaningful, the national movement after independence could no longer remain united. Early in 1959 its radical wing, under Mehdi ben Barka, broke away from an Istiqlal government which it denounced as reactionary, and formed the Union Nationale des Forces Populaires. Moroccan politics since then have developed increasingly as a conflict between the reformers of the UNFP and the new and personally ambitious ruler, King Hassan II, son of the late Muhammad ben Youssef. In July 1963 the king's police began arresting his UNFP opponents, and by the end of the year the Moroccan regime had degenerated into a royal autocracy.

The other territories of the former French empire in North Africa, Algeria and Tunisia, have had different experience. In Tunisia there was no chiefly hierarchy of any importance, but a considerable Tunisian business and farming class. It was the latter, united in the Néo-Destour Party, which led the campaign for independence. After many troubles and a brief armed struggle they triumphed in 1955, opening the way for the Istiqlal in Morocco; and their national movement has remained stable and substantially (though not entirely) united since then, while the shrewd and popular President Bourghiba has had no serious rival.

In Algeria no ruling hierarchy had survived the close attrition of colonial occupation since the 1830s, and no indigenous business class had ever had the chance to emerge. There were a few Muslim leaders of the conservative sort and a handful of wealthy Algerian landowners;* but neither of these could form a significant political grouping. There remained for nationalism, faced

* Of native Algerian landowners, 1 per cent had 21 per cent of the land belonging to Algerians, or an average of about 620 acres each, in 1954. *Cahiers Internationaux*, 1954, no. 64, quoted by I. Potekhin in the *Journal of Modern African Studies*, 1963, Vol. 1, No. 1, Dar-es-Salaam.

by an absolute French determination to treat Algeria as an integral part of France, only the route of insurrection. This was tried several times, and always with disaster until 1954. There then began an insurrection which succeeded after seven terrible years of colonial repression. In 1962 Algeria became an independent republic under the Front de Libération Nationale (FLN), with one of its outstanding leaders, Ahmed Ben Bella, as its first Premier and then President.

Arguing from the experience of examples like these, it may be seen that 'tribalism' has many facets, and that its effective political strength at the point of independence is often, if not always, in direct relation to the policies of the withdrawing colonial Power. Yet it remains a factor of importance on its own. There is 'tribalism' and tribalism. How far the genuine article will remain significant in the years ahead will depend on the manner in which progress is made, or not made, towards building a new society.

10 Working It Out

All the thirty-odd independent governments in Africa are now pledged, if with varying degrees of conviction, to construct more industry, raise standards of living, and provide many other aspects of a modern state. We have sufficiently looked at the reasons for this: the ruin and incapacity of the old way of life; the demand for a new way; the sheer weight of poverty, disease, or boredom; and a sense of profound material inferiority towards the rest of the world. All these and parallel motives have created a public opinion, eager for rapid and even startling change, which no African government can ignore and few can resist.

There is no means yet of knowing how far and quickly these demands will be satisfied. What one can do at present is to trace where the dominant lines of action now point. For this, inevitably, we shall have to select a few countries among many. But it will be important to remember that all of Africa's independent peoples are involved in a process of development or attempted development, even when the stumbling blocks (whether of leadership or social structure) seem most forbidding.

Thus President Tubman of Liberia and the Emperor Haile Selassie of Ethiopia, both of them conservative by character as well as confronted with strong traditional conservatism in the framework of their respective governments, are each engaged in pushing their countries, though by different routes, into the twentieth century. Ethiopia today is no longer the mere feudal structure of a recent past. Modern Liberia is likewise different from the mere 'coastal oligarchy', floated off the rocks of indolence and insolvency by the cash of an American rubber corporation, that President Tubman took over twenty years ago. For while Liberia may remain 'a virtual oligarchy', with 'corruption ... possibly more deeply engrained in the Liberian polity than anywhere else in West Africa', Tubman's policy has been 'an effort to redress the balance of power in favour of the tribal elements of the interior at the expense of the [Negro] settler minority around the capital'.[135]

And since it is true that much of Africa is now in full tide of many-levelled change and upheaval, even the most 'settled' of situations are likely to undergo rapid shifts of speed and direction. Dogmatic conclusions are even less appropriate here than anywhere else. The last four years in the Ivory Coast have seen no determined effort to build a new society, but it would be doing an injustice to Houphouët-Boigny's regime to suggest that the country had undergone no changes at all in that time, or may not undergo others in the near future. It would be wide of the mark to say that Guinea has reached socialism, its stated goal, yet still further astray to maintain that Guinea still lingers at the same primitive stage of post-colonial change as some of the equatorial territories.

The degree and direction of change are obviously governed to a large extent by the 'inherited situation'. One sees this very clearly in North Africa. If it was possible for independent Tunisia to avoid major upheavals, at any rate so far as the basic economic structure of society was concerned – even to the point, indeed, where the national economic plan could be officially described as 'a sort of councilling agency to assist private companies in defining their projects'[136] – this was certainly not the case with Egypt.*

Egypt was a country, characteristic of its semi-colonial type, where the richer were getting richer and the poor poorer at an almost visible annual rate, but where the poor vastly outnumbered the rich. Nothing short of great structural reform could have prevented this society from deepening internal crisis. Much of this reform, duly undertaken by President Nasser's regime in the past ten years, was necessarily in a revolutionary direction: the expropriation of royal and some other large estates, massive public investment in land reclamation and hydraulic works, widespread promotion of forms of peasant

---

* An initial land reform in Tunisia has limited holdings to a maximum size of 50 hectares (110 acres), and in 1963 there were signs of further structural reorganization.

cooperation – these and other such steps were scarcely open to question if the regime was to show any real progress, although this does not mean that they were therefore easy to take.

The question for Nasser then became: what next? Beyond such reforms there was a choice to be made. Nasser's choice of 'Arab socialism' or 'democratic cooperative socialism', as it is variously described in the official press, bears the imprint of many traditions: Muslim conservatism, the mental formation of Egyptian officers, socialist teaching as well as capitalist pressure, but above all, perhaps, the country's ancient habit of highly centralized direction.

By 1962 this particular choice had begun to make itself felt. In some ways it seemed a contradictory sort of choice. The government was claiming to have helped the mass of people by redistributing about ten per cent of the total area under cultivation; but most of the 226,000 families who benefited from this were small rather than landless peasants, and the needs of the latter were barely touched.[137] 'Arab socialism' was claiming to have set the people free; but the prisons were crammed with socialists and, of course, communists. The further question for Nasser then became: could his choice now find ways of stabilizing – and this, in the circumstances, meant democratizing – a new structure imposed from the top, since its capacity for social growth was otherwise all too likely to remain minimal? The year of 1963 brought some interesting answers to this question: among them, indeed, a steady release of political prisoners and a further instalment of social reform, especially on the land. Egypt presents the interesting spectacle of a country where much has lately changed, and much is changing still.

Nothing like this can be said of Morocco. There a 'leftist' foreign policy has appeared to go hand in hand with a general domestic stagnation. No structural reforms of any magnitude have yet occurred in the antiquated landowning and *métayage* systems; French investment capital has dried up and little has yet been found among businessmen at home; while the population is said to have increased by nearly a fifth over the past seven years. Here the 'inherited situation' has continued to obstruct new policies of growth. Morocco is a country which has yet to find its way ahead.

In Algeria, next door, the FLN early declared that its war for independence should bring a complete renewal of society: the sufferings and sacrifices would be justified by nothing less. Radical reorganization of land ownership and land use was high on the programme. Not surprisingly. 'At the beginning of the Algerian Revolution' – November 1954 – 'six million Algerians were living or rather subsisting on an average annual income per head of 16,000 old francs (about £12) ...'[138] This being so, the 'Algerian Revolution ... is not and cannot be a simple fight for the conquest of political power. For us ... it is a political, economic, and social Revolution.'[139] *El Moudjahid*, official journal of the FLN, explained in 1960 that 'the land reform of tomorrow will be necessarily and ineluctably an *agrarian revolution* [italics in original] or it will be nothing'. In December 1961 the journal went further. The reconstruction of Algeria could take place only on the basis of 'a genuine land reform which will allow a progressive structure of landowner-ship', and 'will banish capitalist forms of production by decisively limiting the size of individual property ... Whether within the framework of family holdings, or within that of much larger properties taken in hand by the community, or by the state, we must prepare for the collective organization of farming – alone capable of improving the productivity of the land by the use of modern methods and means of cultivation.'[140]

Taking over a ravaged country from which most of the European landowners had fled, and where thousands of peasants had lost home and livelihood, the newly independent govern-ment headed by Ben Bella had gone some way by the autumn of 1963 to make good these wartime promises. They were helped in this by the voluntary abandonment of French estates in the fertile regions. During the winter of 1962 peasant workers had begun cultivating land left idle by their former employers. In March the government legalized these 'take-overs', covering in all about 3,300,000 acres of the country's best farming country. In the following October Ben Bella declared that 'every hectare' of land belonging to French settlers was now nationalized, thus adding about another 3,000,000 acres to the expropriated total. At the same time it was announced that large Muslim land-owners would also lose some of their property, though it had still to be decided exactly how much. The eventual aim was to bring under public ownership about half of Algeria's cultivable land.

An essential feature of this massive change was that the nationalized estates were not divided among individual peasants but handed to the community of all those who worked on them. These communities formed *assemblés d'autogestion* which in turn elected *comités d'autogestion*, self-management committees; and these, flanked by government-appointed managers, numbered by October as many as 1,800, with others being continually formed.[141] Though suffering from a desperate shortage of cash, mechanics, and book-keepers, and still lacking an efficient administration to take the place of the French, the new machinery of state and of workers' self-management had begun to appear as much more than a promising experiment, and as a possibly crucial move towards socialism.

The FLN had also looked forward to the creation of some basic and some processing industries, together with a large expansion of social and educational services for a people who sorely needed them. While little enough could yet be done in these directions – for the everyday problems of building an administration and repairing war damage were of monumental dimensions – Algeria in 1963 seemed clearly headed for large and constructive changes in its 'inherited structure'.

These North African contrasts in policy and posture are reflected among the countries south of the Sahara, though in a different context of daily life and traditional attitude. Here, too, there is a common point of reference in the emphasis on public investment – on state capitalism – whether for public utilities and services, for raising the productivity of farmers, or for laying the foundations of industry. And here, too, one finds some countries which have 'chosen their way' and others which have not, with wide variations in both categories.

First of all there are the countries which may be grouped from an African standpoint under the heading of the 'not yet free'. Aside from South Africa, these include Southern Rhodesia and the three High Commission Territories (Basutoland, Swaziland, Bechuanaland); South-West Africa (theoretically a United Nations Trusteeship Territory but in practice a colonial

province of South Africa); the three Portuguese colonies –
formally, oversea provinces – of Angola, Moçambique, and
(Portuguese) Guinea; and a scatter of Spanish possessions of
which (Spanish) Guinea – consisting of the island of Fernando
Po and an adjacent mainland enclave called Rio Muni – is the
most important. Besides these, Kenya, Northern Rhodesia,
Nyasaland, and Gambia had yet to achieve full independence
when this book was written.

Secondly, south of the Sahara, there are some ex-French
possessions whose links with France have remained so strong
and numerous as to separate these countries from their more
independent neighbours. It would be wrong, of course, to see
them simply as 'masked colonies'. They are more than that.
While it is true that the four states of the old colonial federation
of French Equatorial Africa – Congo (formerly Moyen Congo),
Central African Republic (formerly Oubangui), Gabon, and
Chad – depend largely on French aid and advice, and are
themselves poor and sparsely populated (all four of them
together having many fewer people than Ghana or the Western
Region of Nigeria), they are governed by shrewd politicians
who have well understood *comment se faire valoir* – a phrase
that may be reasonably translated, at any rate in this context,
as 'how to keep your cake *and* eat it'. Thus the Abbé Fulbert
Youlou, President of Congo (Brazzaville), could be relied upon
to march in step with Paris on all matters of major importance,
but Paris, in return, would generally pay attention to President
Youlou and listen to his needs with a sympathetic ear. How
far his needs were likely to be the same as his country's, of
course, might well be quite another thing.* And the Abbé
Fulbert Youlou was not unique in this respect.

Moreover, these equatorial ex-colonies are still at an early
stage of transition from the 'colonial-traditional' way of life.
They were always the Cinderellas of the French Empire:
milked by concession companies from 1900 until 1930, they
never achieved the comparatively favoured posture of some of
the French West African territories. For this and other reasons
they generally failed to build a strong and stable basis for political

* In August 1963 Youlou, though initially supported by French troops, was
forced by a rioting opposition to retire from the scene – temporarily at least.

sovereignty. Either they lacked broad and popular nationalist parties (as distinct from more or less unorganized movements led by demagogues), or else these parties failed to meet the test of winning effective independence, or else (as notably in Kamerun) they fell apart and fought each other.

In a third group are several countries, among them some of the weightiest on the continent, which have acquired full political sovereignty but not, as yet, any clear choice of route into the future. These I have called 'the unresolved', though the label must not be tied too tightly on any of them. Lastly, there are a few countries whose policies and practices put them into a fourth group, which I have labelled 'the committed'.

These labels, needless to say, are mainly for the sake of convenience. Yet even though it is true that all states in Africa (or anywhere else) are 'unresolved', since they will all undergo continuous evolution in the future, it is also true that some are notably 'more resolved' than others, and are indeed 'committed' to specific policies of social growth. This distinction is, as will be seen, important.

The Unresolved

At first sight the countries in this group often give the appearance of enduring stability and inner self-confidence. In some ways this appearance reflects the truth. Yet in other ways the signs now begin to suggest that their situation contains an inner crisis of development, a political and economic lack of balance, which have yet to take their full effect. These 'unresolved' countries, or rather their governments, may believe that they have chosen their route into the future: what seems far from certain is that the route in question can or will lead sufficiently far from the starting-point to satisfy the general expectation.

Among the ex-French countries, the Ivory Coast is prominent among 'the unresolved'. Its apparent prosperity conceals a static social condition – an opposition between an African plantocracy and the labour it employs – whose further movement seems at present threatened with paralysis by heavy dependence on the French market and a consequent reliance on 'things remaining as they are'.

But Nigeria is the crucial example. The most populous and in some ways the most exciting country in all Africa, this great federation is remarkable for its rich history, range of traditional wisdom, variety of energetic populations, and actual or potential wealth in soil and oil and minerals. To begin with, Nigeria is already a success. It is extraordinary, after all, that Nigeria should exist at all, for Nigeria contains three major regions of which each has a population as large as or even much larger than many African states. Had these three regions fallen to the 'tutelage' of different European powers, or within different colonial frontiers, they could scarcely have come together. Each has strong characteristics of its own. Each has a long and in many respects sovereign history of its own – the history of Yorubaland in the West, of the Hausa, Bornu, and Fulani states in the North, of those of the Niger Delta and the Ibo in the East. Within all three regions there are many lesser contrasts, so many indeed that political programmes have spoken of the need to 'regionalize' Nigeria into a dozen or even more autonomous states. If the same ideas had governed British policy in Nigeria during the pre-independence years as governed British policy in Kenya during the same period, Nigeria might indeed have embarked on independence as a cluster of statelets whose respect for a central authority was little more than nominal.

But Nigerian nationalism during the 1950s – most characteristically in the work and writings of Nnamdi Azikiwe – desired unity; and this proved decisive. That in itself was much, and it may be unrealistic to have expected any more. The major effort at winning independence within a Nigerian framework, coupled with the often ticklish problems of combining this with a reasonable measure of regional autonomy, occupied all energies.

The Sardauna of Sokoto put this point with his usual graceful irony when writing, in his autobiography, of the problems of political growth.

So far, none of the 'political' parties have produced programmes markedly different from each other. ... The reason is simple. In the old days, when the British were the 'government', all parties concentrated on demanding self-government to the exclusion of all

149

else. .... Attacking the existing government was the main occupation, and it was not particularly difficult and did not demand any real thought. Naturally, when the British withdrew gradually, and the power passed, there was no one to attack and, as we had got self-government, there was nothing more to be said about it. So far no burning question has arisen on which we are likely to take sides strongly.

The upshot, as an American investigator, Professor Bretton of Michigan University, has lately written, is that Nigeria has come to independence 'without any real ideology, even a negative one, in its ruling circles'.[142] This seems also to be true of Sierra Leone, a country which deserves far closer attention than space will allow here.

These Nigerian 'ruling circles' in any case found it difficult to see the present in terms of dynamic transition to a different future. They were heavily weighted on the traditional and conservative side of African life, especially in the North, where power had passed largely into the hands of the traditional Fulani emirs – much less open to democratic pressure, as the Sardauna of Sokoto has lately pointed out,[143] than in pre-British times – and in the West, where that subtle nexus of political and commercial interest represented by the enterprising chiefs of Yorubaland had remained the real seat of authority. This innately conservative pattern of political life, clothed now with the institutions of Westminster parliamentarianism, has misled many non-Africans into imagining that Nigeria is, in fact, really no different from a rather poor though promising member of the West European community of nations. Hence it came as a bitter disappointment when the 'most promising' of all the regional governments, that of the go-ahead West whose leaders had shown so many signs of embracing 'Western civilization', broke down in 1963, a state of emergency was declared, un-savoury scandals reached the light of day, and all seemed back in the melting pot again.

Some critics seized this opportunity to speak glumly of a 'reversion to tribalism'. This seems to me another misunder-standing. It is hard to see how the word 'tribalism' can be applied to a country like Yorubaland, where a sense of nation-hood has long existed; aside from this, the trouble surely lay (and lies) deeper than disruptions caused by local loyalties in conflict with central government. The crisis, essentially, was not of 'tribe against tribe', but of traditional modes of political life at grips with modern problems and demands.

Individuals were partly to blame. It was manifestly true, as the Coker Commission showed, that a number of people in Nigeria's 'ruling circles' saw their country not as a society to be passionately believed in, but – the words are Bretton's – 'one which was more of a vehicle for personal advancement'. Others saw it as a vehicle for conserving customary forms of hierarchical power. Yet these individual attitudes were merely the personal reflection of a national problem. Could traditional modes of political life, even though modified by parliamentary processes, possibly avail to shift Nigeria out of her poverty and ignorance into the leading position she could undoubtedly aspire to claim? Falling standards of living for many people in the towns, far too slow an advance in the countryside, haphazard or superficial planning: all these seemed to answer in the negative. This vast and many-sided country certainly enjoyed a high measure of stability; but the stability appeared to have come perilously near stagnation. And nobody seemed to have any clear or consistent policy for getting on the move again.

Towards 1963, accordingly, Nigeria grew discontented with herself. 'Today,' wrote a distinguished Nigerian schoolmaster and journalist, 'one thing is clear in the minds of the young elements in our country – Nigeria is not being effectively governed. Our government is a hydra-headed octopus that veers and backs, depending on the prevailing planetary and political winds, and that oscillates and flounders and hopes, whatever happens, for the best. It is not purposive; it is not logical; it is not disciplined.'[144] Another well-known Nigerian journalist, Gabriel Fagbure (Lagos *Sunday Times*, 15 December 1963), wrote of 'the appalling mismanagement of our public affairs, the lack of sense of direction on the national level, the moral depravity of our society . . .

London's most consistently intelligent commentary on Nigerian affairs put it more gently: 'The real crisis in Nigeria is its unique experiment of meeting the challenges of a new, vast, multi-tribal state in Africa with all the borrowed apparatus of Western democracy. Nigerians are now deciding whether this structure should be modified or whether they can, after all, make it work as it is.'[145] In other words, the central 'problem of power' was resolved for the time being, but resolved in a conservative sense; and yet this solution, though often locally effective, appeared no longer capable of facing the severe challenge of carrying Nigeria fully into the modern world.

One sees all this most clearly in Nigerian ideas about planning for development. Some forms of planning had been undertaken by the British, and with positive results. By the end of 1952-3 a total of £28·5 millions had been spent under Nigerian programmes of the Colonial Development and Welfare Scheme, just over half of which had come from Nigerian sources.[146] But this was planning of a primitive sort, limited to little more than raising funds and spending them on desirable objectives, stopping far short of the principles of a planned economy which were to emerge later. There was to be state enterprise and private enterprise, but which was to control the other? The question was crucial in deciding the shape and direction of Nigeria's economic growth; but it was not asked.

'We intend,' declared an Eastern Region planning report of 1955, 'that statutory corporations should be created with the idea of administering certain new and complex functions for which civil-service organization is inadequate whilst, on the other hand, private enterprise is too mercenary and profit-seeking.' But this report could none the less recommend the creation of a Finance Corporation which should make 'liberal advances to hard-pressed business organizations'.[147] And the same ambivalent attitude to the vital question of economic control, to the choice of direction – *either* towards state capitalism leading into socialism *or* towards state capitalism leading into 'free enterprise' – governed the later and much larger all-Nigeria economic plan of 1962.

It was a valuable aspect of this ambitious plan that the lion's share of responsibility and spending should lie with the federal government, whose authority and influence would be correspondingly reinforced to the advantage of Nigerian unity. But the plan itself was on the old 'shopping list' lines. Its root idea seems to have been that state investment should pave the way for private investment. Great hopes were placed in stimulating the growth of private business among Nigerians: a sum of £4 millions, for example, was allocated to the establishment of a Development Bank 'in which private Nigerian investors, foreign private investors, and the International Bank and its affiliates will, it is hoped, participate'. Meanwhile, large industrial and utility projects were planned for which the state (whether by federal or regional government) and foreign capital would join in common effort. Of the total projected sum of £676 millions to be spent in development over six years, foreign aid was to provide £339 millions, or just over half.[148]

This was an almost classical application of a British concept dominant during the fifties. A responsible 'middle class' should take over power, operating through parliamentary institutions as nearly like those of Westminster as possible, and should promote its country's interests by advancing its own. By such means, Nigeria would emerge within a few years as a stable democracy founded not only on the patterns of Westminster but, much more important, on the reality of a flourishing middle class. This middle class would remould Nigerian institutions – pushing ahead with education, developing industries and communications, laying 'tribalism' finally on the shelf – and would become, in so doing, a bastion of the Western way of life.

But can it happen that way? Isn't this precisely an extension of what Bretton has shrewdly called the 'new myth of wishful thinking' about Nigeria which has grown up in Europe and North America – the myth which 'mistakes the community of interests between the leading Western countries and a group of Nigerian leaders oriented towards the *status quo* for a valid formula to cope with Nigeria's problems'? In order to be a 'valid formula' of this kind, Nigeria's middle class would have to be large, coherent, inured to political responsibility, and widely spread throughout the regions.

Now the middle class of Nigeria may be in a healthier condition than most 'middle classes' in Africa, but it is scarcely any of these things in adequate measure, while recent events in the Western Region suggest that its readiness for political responsibility may too often fall short of the most minimal requirement. And while parallels with Europe or South America may quickly mislead, a good deal of experience has shown that representative government cannot be reconciled with the rule of a financial and commercial oligarchy – even if Nigeria's middle class can as yet claim to have reached that status. There would seem to be a real danger that the present system of power in Nigeria, evidently aiming now at the promotion of a middle class which is to dominate the country, must either run aground on its own incapacity or else, provoked by growing popular pressure for a better life which it cannot quickly provide, open the road to autocratic forms of rule. Here again one may question whether a *democratic* installation and early growth of capitalism can be any more possible in Nigeria than it was in Europe.

It remains true that Nigeria has moved significantly in the past few years. Primary as well as secondary education has achieved great strides in the two southern regions, and begun to do the same in the more conservative north; while the Plan, whatever its basic failings, takes good care to provide plenty of money (potentially at least) for medical and other services. Universities are going ahead with help from the United States and elsewhere, and with much drive and enthusiasm at home. Yet the very success of Nigeria's widely spreading educational facilities has acutely raised the problem of development. A record number of children left primary school in the Eastern Region last year; but how many could be sure of finding a quick road to skilled employment, or even any gainful employment? The answer is suggested by experience in the Western Region. Of about 100,000 children leaving primary school every year in the Western Region, a White Paper of 1963 pointed out, only half 'gain admission into other schools for further education, *or find useful employment*' (my italics).

This is one cause for worry that has lately led Nigerians to question the 'middle-class' theory of growth. It is not difficult to understand their doubts. By the methods of 'free enterprise' – of promoting a large and responsible middle class through state capitalism and foreign private investment – the building of a 'welfare economy' must clearly take a long time, even (on precedents abroad) a very long time. Yet it is time, precisely, that remains in short supply. Aside from the question of post-primary employment, there is the even more pressing problem of what happens to the large numbers of young men and women whom the country's multiplying secondary schools are now turning out every year. These young folk may be excused for wanting well-paid 'nine-to-five' jobs in city commerce and the professions; yet what the country really needs of them is low-paid service in humble schools and remote villages. But the familiar pressures of middle-class formation in an economy of 'booming individualism' continually present them with the glittering ideal of the *personal career*, and, by so doing, continually devalue the ideal of service to the community in favour of service to self.

Aside from this question of service, however vital to continued social and economic growth, there is another pressing problem. What are these young folk going to do and think when they cannot find the *personal careers* to which they have been led to believe themselves entitled? Will they really be content to put their certificates into a drawer along with their white collars and ties and neat blouses, and labour quietly at low-paid work until the slow processes of capital-formation and investment have provided what the economists call 'take off' – have fired that swift and sudden rise to higher standards which are possible, or should be possible, once the infra-structure of industrial development is laid? Putting it another way, how do you achieve an atmosphere of social service in a system geared to personal advancement?

In a somewhat different direction, it is relevant to such questions that a great deal of planned development is to be provided by the investment of state-accumulated reserves from various forms of taxation and marketing-board activity. A sound and necessary policy: but are those farmers whose work has created these reserves, or a large part of them, really going to be content to see them concentrated on the building of a commercial and industrial middle class? And if not, what influence may such pressures bring to bear on Nigeria's sometimes precarious structure of parliamentary government? The private interests of a small minority – and this is what a middle class must here remain for a long time to come – may easily come to seem incompatible with the interests of the majority of people, especially when, as in Nigeria, these people include so many men and women of enterprise, initiative, and intelligence.

These and similar doubts and self-questionings are not the least interesting aspect of the political atmosphere in Nigeria. Their existence should not suggest, of course, that some vast groundswell of revolution is now surging beneath the surface of Nigerian life. If that were so the situation would be far less calm and stable than it actually is. But it would be evidently optimistic to imagine that the everyday composure of Nigerians – for the most part, a people of unusual self-confidence and faith – provides any guarantee that Nigeria is set upon a course which can solve her problems of transition. It is more likely to be true that Nigeria remains, in respect of what her people will decide or not decide, Africa's great unknown.

Uganda offers much the same conclusion in East Africa. Here too a central government under a skilful leader, Mr Milton Obote, has battled to maintain and promote its authority over traditional kings and old divisive loyalties. Here too an ambitious development plan may give the central government a crucial accession of authority in dealing with the autonomous ambitions of a ruler as locally powerful as the Kabaka of Buganda. And here too an industrious farming community offers a solid foundation for progress, provided that the structures built on this foundation are the right ones. What should these be? For the moment, nobody seems to have gone very far in thinking about this. Education, hygiene, water-power, some industry: all these are clearly needed. But for what kind of society? It may be unrealistic to expect Mr Obote and his colleagues to answer such questions at this early stage. No doubt they feel that long-term solutions for Uganda must depend quite largely on what happens to the project for East African Federation.

Ethiopia is another 'unresolved' regime, but with a difference. In one sense, of course, Ethiopia is highly 'resolved': the emperor rules by personal decision through a centralized bureaucracy and a network of more or less loyal vassals. And in the last few years the present emperor has done much to strengthen his government's authority. If a good deal of the country remains beyond his everyday control, this is largely a reflection of the feudal past: his predecessors had the custom, altogether necessary to their rule, of moving through Ethiopia from one region to another, putting down revolts, reassuring themselves of vassal fealty, holding courts, and promulgating laws. Compared with that not-distant past, the Emperor Haile Selassie has major achievements to his credit. He has done a good deal to weld the country together. He has endowed it with a sprinkle of modern schools and a university in his capital. He reigns as something like an autocrat, but it would be completely unrealistic to imagine that he could solve his 'problem of power' in any other way: a reporter of the B.B.C. who lately asked him if he could not now envisage handing over some of his power to representatives of the people had simply misunderstood the nature of politics.[149] Ethiopia has as yet no democratic parties which could bear the weight of that responsibility.

In another sense, though, Ethiopia is plainly a country in movement towards new forms of social life. A recent revolt against the emperor's authority may or may not have betokened democratic awakening – the facts are obscure – but it certainly showed that the notion of modernization, which the present emperor has steadfastly followed in his own cautious way, is seeping down to the new young men whose education belongs to the 1950s. Over and beyond this, there is the influence of change, and demand for change, among Ethiopia's neighbours near and far. Here again it has been Haile Selassie who first grasped the point. By attaching Ethiopia firmly to the campaign for African unity, he has thoroughly involved his people in African affairs for the first time in many centuries. In so doing he has probably opened up some useful avenues for progress at home. There may be no democratic revolution in the foreseeable future; there is none the less likely to be continued movement towards new and more expansive patterns of society.

The Committed

It may be said of a few countries in Africa that they are consciously committed to the building of a radically different kind of society from the one they inherited. Mainly, their commitment is towards socialism. Does this mean that they are really camouflaged satellites of the Soviet Union or China? Not in the least: the familiar Western fear of communism in Africa ignores the fact that Africans want to solve their own problems in their own way. What 'commitment' here implies, I think, is that leaders and parties mean to use the machinery of state capitalism, linked to the growth of cooperatives and a renewed sense of service to the community, as a means of development not towards the growth of a favoured middle class but towards the active involvement of large masses of people in a deliberate effort at political and economic democracy.

How one regards these various efforts will partly depend on what they do, but also on who one is. 'Ghanaians comprehend representative government,' *Time* remarked with effortless condescension not long ago, 'but Moscow-leaning Kwame Nkrumah misrules [his] country as [an] autocracy.'[150] Yet a few months later another prominent American magazine, the *Atlantic Monthly*, had concluded that 'on paper, the Ghana program seems no more socialistic than Nigeria's $1·8 billion six-year plan of development. But there is a huge difference in atmosphere. Nigeria in some ways resembles nineteenth-century America, with foreign capitalists rushing in, hoping for quick profits, and with land bloating in value. Although the state plans a good deal of supervision and interference, the Nigerian economy basically is capitalist in atmosphere.'

'Ghana is different,' continued the *Atlantic Monthly*. 'While Nkrumah has kept nationalization (with liberal compensation) to a minimum, Ghana is committed to a socialist future. It has a calm, ordered atmosphere and moves in a disciplined way ...' No mention of 'autocracy' here: on the contrary, Nigeria and Ghana 'may be proceeding in the only economic way possible. And Ghana's way, because of its size, may be the easiest.'[151]

The notions of 'capitalism' and 'socialism' are of course relative. Africans often emphasize this. Thus the late Dunduza Chisiza of Nyasaland (Malawi) told an American audience that 'the chances of either of these systems being adopted in an un-adulterated form are very slim'.[152] But the need for *choice*, as we have seen earlier in this book, is not relative: it is an absolute element in the situation. By making a clear choice in favour of a radical reconstruction of society – one that can draw the vast majority of people into active and conscious participation – the 'committed countries' tend to show a stability and solidity which their neighbours seldom share.

Failure to understand this commitment has led to many disappointments in Europe and North America. In Julius Nyerere, for example, the governments of the West have generally seen a man who, they believed, would take a predictable road towards modelling Tanganyika on examples proffered by themselves. There, if anywhere, parliamentary democracy and free-enterprise would surely flourish? Yet within a year of independence Nyerere had declared Tanganyika a one-party state vowed to socialism.

With no money in the till, and almost no 'launching aid' from Britain, an impoverished Tanganyikan government had one card to play. This was political unity. By a tremendous effort in the middle and late fifties, the Tanganyika African National Union had won the adherence of nearly all Africans and not a few among the European and Asian minorities. By 1963 TANU was not only the party of central government – with a virtual monopoly of parliamentary representatives – but had become, in a literal sense, the whole of government in Tanganyika, even down to occupying junior posts in the administration.

The logic of this was clear enough. If the hundred-odd peoples of Tanganyika could unite for large political objectives, what agency except TANU could keep them united? And how could TANU do this unless it were not only the central government and parliament – far-away abstractions in Dar-es-Salaam for most of the country's two million peasant and fisherman families – but also the day-to-day village and regional government as well? There were great and simple difficulties to be faced. There was acute shortage of cash, partly because of natural disasters and partly because of failure to pay taxes (itself a consequence of peasant expectation that 'everything must be different' after independence). In the train of all this, hard decisions had to be taken and realized. That was the work of the administration. Yet the administration, in 1960, was much the same in personnel – or so it would have appeared to the average peasant – as the colonial administration before it.

Unless TANU were to be associated with this administration – were even to *become* this administration – unpopular but necessary decisions could scarcely be carried through. Little by little, Nyerere and his colleagues were driven to the conclusion, fully embraced at the end of 1961, that TANU must not only govern but must also administer. A year later this process was almost complete. The political party and the civil service had, in large degree, become one and the same organization.

This radical solution of Tanganyika's 'problem of power' carried obvious dangers. Who was to control the controllers, once parliament and administration were so closely identified? Occasional abuse of power and some patently wrong appointments soon raised this question to a national issue. Early in 1963 the TANU national committee – by then the country's effective parliament – began casting round for 'checks and balances'. Nyerere, for example, proposed that TANU members might stand in opposition to TANU official candidates at parliamentary elections. He argued that this was advisable since no non-TANU candidates had any chance of being elected, such was the party's popularity at village level. A more serious danger seemed to lie in the general lack of political ideology: it was hard to see how TANU could keep safely moving forward if it lacked a set of rules for navigation. In 1963 Nyerere began to propound some rules for the achievement of African socialism. These, it must be said, do not yet go very far.

But the system also bore some powerful advantages, at least for the time being. It dispensed with the waste and frivolity of political conflicts whose reality was nothing more than personal ambition or clannish conservatism. While Kenya next-door was busy dividing itself into ever smaller units of 'tribal nationalism' – to borrow again Miss Arendt's phrase about Europe – Tanganyika's many peoples remained solidly united. Moreover, the system evolved by TANU put politicians in the best possible posture for behaving as good men: it made them publicly responsible, in short, for the day-to-day application at village level of the decisions they had taken in Dar-es-Salaam. They could blame their failures only on themselves.

This encouraged serious hard work in contrast with the nest-feathering so common in some other countries.

If the system was sound, what about the programme? This, as I have suggested, was still vague and uncertain. 'We are popular now,' a TANU leader commented to me at the end of 1962. 'At the worst, we'll go on being popular for quite some years yet. So don't let's rush things and blunder into nonsense. Let's build calmly.' The obvious good sense of that is reflected in Nyerere's own pronouncements. Later on, a lack of detailed plans can only lead to serious danger; for the moment, it is probably a strength. Tentatively, pragmatically, Tanganyika's ideologists – and this means, really, Nyerere and the TANU national committee – are feeling their way towards a new framework.

Drive through the wide central plains of Tanganyika and you will cross long miles of arid country where villages and homesteads lie few and far between. One of Nyerere's ideas for socialism in Tanganyika is to draw together these villages and homesteads into pockets of good land where the state can concentrate its meagre resources on providing water and social services, and thus the basis for a better life. 'I can't hope to sink a well for every homestead, nor give every peasant a tractor,' he said to me on one occasion, 'but what I can do is to give these things to *groups* of homesteads and farmers. We'll say to such groups – here's watered land, here's a school, roads of access, a tractor. Use them together. Turn yourselves into a producers' cooperative.' Much the same pragmatic attitude has governed the state's acquisition of a half-holding in Tanganyika's diamond mines, and much the same approach may be adopted, as opportunity comes along, to the large sisal and other plantations that are owned by Europeans and Asians but worked by cheap African labour. Though without a precisely detailed plan as yet, Tanganyika is a country committed to social change.

Three countries in West Africa – Ghana, Guinea, and Mali – have moved further in the same general direction. But Ghana must have most of our attention, for it is the most important of the three. With just over seven million people, Ghana is one of Africa's smaller countries. In terms of wealth, social and political cohesion, and dynamic leadership, however, it is well out ahead of almost all the field. In more ways than one it is a pace-maker, a position which seldom makes for popularity, perhaps, but may none the less command attention and respect.

Ghana has also been independent Africa's biggest surprise. If any country should have been content to settle down under a 'new middle class', this was surely the one. With more than £200 millions of sterling assets on the day of independence, an average standard of living that was probably somewhat higher than in Portugal, and a numerous trading community whose contacts with Europe had more than four centuries of varied experience behind them, the new government might surely have sat back in 1957 and happily let things slide.

Yet Ghana today is well launched on a far-reaching programme of social reconstruction, industrialization, and modernization on a radical plan; her overall productivity is vastly higher than it was eight years ago; large new investments are in hand; while 'domestic fixed-capital-formation' is said to have as much as doubled since 1956. Estimated at £532 millions in 1962, Ghana's gross national product has risen to an outstandingly high point for ex-colonial Africa. The slipshod days of early independence, when personal fortunes mushroomed in a boom of corruption and careerism, have given way to a notably different atmosphere. Why and how has this come about?

At the usual risk of over-simplification, one can reply that the story begins with the efforts of Kwame Nkrumah and a handful of like-minded young nationalists to transform the United Gold Coast Convention from a staidly respectable pressure-group of elderly lawyers and chiefs into a 'party of the masses'. That was in 1949. Denounced and rejected with dismay by the leaders of the UGCC, Nkrumah and his friends broke away altogether, formed the Convention People's Party, won mass support up and down the country and turned in 1950 to 'positive action'.[153] They were put in prison for this but released a year later when elections gave decisive victory to the CPP. Nkrumah became the leader of a Gold Coast government with limited domestic powers. Following on their experience with India, Britain's Labour government were ready for a gradual but

decisive transfer of power. Nkrumah's great achievement lay
not only in forcing the pace but, even more, in drawing very
large numbers of ordinary people into political action. There
thus emerged a widely democratic basis for independence.

Full sovereignty was conceded in 1957. What was the position
then? Politically, the new regime had one great asset and one
great liability. Its asset was its widespread popularity with the
common man and his wife, the latter no mean factor in any
part of West Africa. Its liability was a corresponding un-
popularity with all the important chiefs of the inland country,
who rightly saw the CPP as a potent threat to their traditional
influence and privilege. Few leading chiefs wanted independence;
some opposed it vigorously. I remember being received by one
of these in the 'throne room' of his large old country house a
few days before independence. His mood was one of sadness. He
saw no good in what was happening. 'Ah, my boy,' he said,
shaking his handsome old head, 'it all began with that man
Creech-Jones.' He shrugged. 'Now we have a gentleman in
charge, Mr Lennox-Boyd. He will try to do the right thing. But
it is too late, too late.'*

The first independent government, therefore, began life
with a tough challenge to its authority, and this challenge was
made even tougher with the encouragement given to traditional
chiefs, especially in Ashanti, by an independence constitution
which allowed for the formation of strong regional governments.
The object of the chiefly opposition was now to secure a transfer
of power to the regions at the expense of the central government in Accra. Whether he wanted it or not, Nkrumah was thus
faced with an unavoidable choice: either he must break the
power of the principal chiefs, or else resign himself to being
little more than a figurehead. It was very much the situation
that Kenyatta and his colleagues would be required to face in
Kenya seven years later.

Had Nkrumah been a weaker man, or one who believed less
fervently in his mission to take Africans altogether out of their
'second-class citizenship' in the world, he might have accepted

* Mr Arthur Creech-Jones had been Secretary of State for the Colonies in
Britain's post-war Labour government; in 1957 Britain had a Conservative government and Mr Alan Lennox-Boyd was Colonial Secretary.

the comfortable role assigned to him by a regionalist constitution. In that case there can be little doubt that Ghana would have split away into three or four conflicting regions, most of whose leaders would have done their best to conserve the *status quo*. But the *status quo* was precisely what a large number of ordinary folk wanted somehow to change.

This being so, it was possible for Nkrumah and the CPP to quell the opposition of the principal chiefs. They really united the country. Deprived of any far-reaching local power, the regions found themselves under a single government. This was to be the foundation for every major advance the country has since achieved. It was not done easily or peacefully. There were months and even years of sporadic violence or near-violence in Ashanti. But when it was over, surprisingly few had died. And while Ghana has political prisoners today, she has yet to have her first political execution, although a new wave of terror-bombing, aimed especially at Nkrumah began in 1962.

Only those who prefer that Ghana should have remained a congeries of traditional little statelets with no effective central power can fairly criticize Nkrumah's policy of unification. Yet the curious fact remains that many otherwise thoughtful people in Europe and North America have none the less interpreted this policy as one of dictatorship, while some Western newspapers have quite recklessly plastered the government's reputation with accusations of 'autocracy' and the like. This badgering of Ghana has sometimes reached an astonishing point. Not long ago, for example, the head of the department of East European studies at London University felt able to compare Nkrumah's government with the racialist dictatorship of the Afrikaner National Party in South Africa. 'The Labour Party [if it accedes to power] has promised action against South Africa, whose government subjects Africans to political persecution,' wrote Professor H. Seton-Watson to *The Times*, which gave his letter prominence. 'It has yet to announce its intentions towards Ghana, whose government also subjects Africans to political persecution.'[154] To place the breaking of an often violent and reactionary separatist minority in a new state on the same level as the behaviour of Verwoerd's regime in South Africa – under which one fifth of the population is intended to remain complete and permanent master of the other four-fifths – might seem a comical misunderstanding of the truth if it came from a less portentous source. The effect of such criticism in Ghana, of course, is to lead a large number of Ghanaians to believe that influential persons in Britain simply do not want Ghana to make a success of independence.

Having united the country, what next? By about 1959 it once again appeared that the CPP leadership would be content to settle into peaceful comfort, of which, by now, they had plenty. Yet the same mass pressures which had made unity possible now thrust the country forward into a new direction. No doubt Nkrumah's socialist convictions played their part: they could have availed for little, however, if standing still had seemed possible or easy. But it did not. Certainly there was progress. Cocoa-farmers' incomes rose from about £27 millions in 1957, according to official figures, to £48 millions in 1960, while the (official) cost-of-living index rose only from 106 (1954 = 100) to 112. Yet wages stagnated at a low level; and popular demand for higher living standards now began to take the form of open discontent. Besides that, the writing on the wall was anything but hopeful even for the maintenance of existing standards within the *status quo*: cocoa prices might still be high, but the terms-of-trade had been moving decisively against Ghana (as against every primary producer) since the middle fifties. Very large sums were being spent on the import of food, let alone of manufactured goods. And there were here, of course, the same acute problems of post-school employment as in Nigeria. 'Despite the stupendous increase in output,' an official circular commented with an admirable frankness, 'the country is only running in order to stand still.' Once more the CPP leadership was faced with an ultimate choice between abdication (or reduction to dictatorship) and movement forward to a large expansion of the economy. It chose to move forward.

It moved decisively in 1962 with the promulgation of a seven-year development plan which was much more than a mere list of desirable targets and possible donors. This provided for a large expansion of the state-capitalist sector, abandoned previous and vain attempts to 'make local capitalists do the job', and placed primary emphasis on raising agricultural productivity together with a major effort in many sectors at transforming a one-crop economy (based on cocoa) into a diversified and industrial complex. In contrast with other countries which had also opted for a measure of state capitalism, here the 'state capitalist content' was projected specifically into a socialist framework.

'Socialism,' Nkrumah told a meeting of CPP organizers in April 1961, 'is the only pattern that can within the shortest possible time bring the good life to the people ... [but] all talk of socialism, of economic and social reconstruction, is just empty words if we do not seriously address ourselves to the question of basic industrialization and agricultural revolution in our country ...'[155]

From about this time the government made new and successful efforts at buying up important foreign concerns, notably in gold-mining, and laid down careful conditions under which future private investment could be made. Founded half a century earlier, the gold-mining companies had realized their original investment many times over. Until 1944 they had remained 'with no levy on their exports other than insignificant rents to the chief and a slight tax to the government. All income tax was paid within England itself.'[156] About half the gross income of the mines went year by year, as we have seen, almost untaxed abroad. After 1944 small domestic taxes were imposed, and these were later somewhat increased.

But with 1960 the government moved into the mining field itself. It purchased five mining companies in the Tarkwa region at a cost of £5½ millions, a fairly generous but shrewd transaction which cost about the value of one year's annual output of gold; and today Ghana's state mining corporation produces just over half of the country's gold. Although rather more than half of total diamond production remains in foreign hands, diamond dealing has been transferred to Accra with a consequent effect on revenue. Among other purchases was the large Leventis retail-marketing concern, for which £6 millions were paid; and a beginning has since been made in state retail-trading through 'people's shops', under the direction, interestingly enough, of a former senior British executive of the United

Africa Company. In farming meanwhile, the 'agricultural stations' of former days were transformed into more than a hundred state farms; unemployed men were absorbed into many other farms run by the Ghana Workers' Brigade; and there was a wide and evidently very popular extension of cooperative marketing and production.

At the same time a large proportion of sterling reserves, accumulated under the colonial regime and held for a long time as 'blocked balances' in London, have been used in primary development, notably in completing a new deep-water harbour and township at Tema, east of Accra, at the cost of nearly £30 millions, and in preliminary work on the huge Volta dam at Akosombo, still in progress, towards which Ghana is contributing £35 millions and which will be of great industrial importance.[157] Much other money is going into the improvement of farming methods, fertilizers, and types of seed.

Ghana has also taken its 'neutralism' seriously and to active purpose. After some hesitations, the United States and other Western official lenders are devoting no less than £93 millions to the Volta dam and its connected enterprises, whether in hydro-electric power or the mining and processing of bauxite, while the Soviet Union is building another dam on the Volta and has granted credits worth about £29 millions for repayment in ten years at $2\frac{1}{2}$ per cent, the repayment to be largely by the proceeds of Ghanaian exports, or, in other words, cocoa. Other communist countries have agreed to comparable credits on a smaller scale. The objective of all these Eastern agreements has been agricultural and industrial diversification, with payment in cocoa. 'The Eastern bloc are paying for this cocoa at the rate of 55 per cent in hard currency and 45 per cent in goods and services . . . [They have] guaranteed Ghana a total of £100 millions in credits for new industries to be planned and eventually built by their own technicians.'[158]

A consistent policy towards private investment has also been projected. The government would henceforth recognize 'five sectors, all operating side by side in the nation's economy. These sectors are:

1. State enterprises.
2. Enterprises owned by foreign private interests.

3. Enterprises jointly owned by the state and foreign private interests.
4. Cooperatives.
5. Small-scale Ghanaian enterprises.'[159]

It seems clear from this that state-controlled enterprise is to dominate the economy. But while thus pointing the economy away from 'free enterprise', the government have taken some care to welcome foreign private investors who might be prepared to cooperate on acceptable terms. 'All enterprises,' that is to say, would be 'expected to accept the economic policy of the government as the basis of their activity.'[160] In mid-1963 the Ghanaian ambassador to the United States assured a business audience in Washington that 'foreign investors had nothing to fear in Ghana'.[161]

Part of this new attitude to private investment has consisted in an attempt to persuade foreign companies to invest some of their profits in the processing of locally produced raw material. Some large firms have quickly agreed. In 1963, for example, the United Africa Company (Unilever) built a soap-and-toothpaste factory in Ghana at the cost of £2 million. This plant, commented Nkrumah when opening it, was proof of a new relationship with foreign investors. In the past Unilever had bought palm-oil in Africa and brought it back again as soap made in Europe. 'Now the wheel has turned full circle, and Lever Brothers, who originally came to Ghana for the raw material, are today manufacturing here the finished product.' In this way, as well as by public investment, Ghana's narrow 'industrial base' was being steadily broadened.

By 1964, accordingly, the pressures for a better life could begin to be met, if cautiously, with solid claims to have opened out the future. Though events in the political field might now – perhaps inevitably – take an increasingly abrupt and controversial turn, there could be little doubt that Ghana was moving towards a new and stable economic basis. What could be argued for the regime, indeed, was that it had squarely faced the challenge of large-scale economic reconstruction as well as of social change; that it had scored a number of outstanding initial successes; and that with hard work and a measure of good fortune Ghanaians could now hope within a fairly short time to see their country vastly more resilient, wealthy, and agreeable to live in than before. If the dangers inherent in single party rule could be avoided, this now seemed to many thoughtful observers the principal reality about Ghana. The British High Commissioner, Sir Geoffrey de Freitas, was more than merely courteous when he opined in 1963 that 'of all tropical African countries, Ghana has the best prospects economically'.[162] Views like this, true enough, have seldom been reflected in the press of Europe and North America; but the 'gap in sympathy' between Ghana – and indeed most of Africa – and much of the Western press had now grown ominously wide.

A detailed comparison between Ghana and its two socialist-orientated allies in West Africa, Guinea and Mali, would show some similarities and some startling differences. Broadly, though, all three are moving in much the same direction and by much the same means. The policy of all three is based on a belief that ex-colonial countries can and should rebuild their economies on a non-capitalist basis, and that failure to achieve this will lead only to new if indirect forms of colonial subjection.

With a population less than half of Ghana's (and a little smaller than Mali's) Guinea achieved independence in late 1958 with the handicap of acute rural poverty and alongside a complete rupture with France. The French departed suddenly, cutting off all aid, facilities, and good will. In this absolute break with the colonial power there lay an immediate gain to which Sékou Touré and the Parti Démocrate de la Guinée were by no means blind. They could proceed without further hindrance to a radical reform of the whole spirit as well as personnel of the administration. Their Ghanaian contemporaries, by contrast, had often complained of Britain's slowness to move. Yet the disadvantages soon became apparent. Guinea sorely lacked capital and trained men. Knowing this, the newly independent government tried from the first to restore friendship with Paris (to which many of their members and intellectuals were in any case emotionally committed), though this was to prove possible only in 1963. In their helpless isolation, meanwhile, they turned for help to those who would give it. They forged new and valuable links with Ghana, but also with the Soviet Union and some other communist countries.

By the end of 1960 they were running into fresh difficulties, largely caused by trying to go too far too fast. They overstrained their resources in experienced manpower, available capital, and popular political understanding; and they planned on a level that proved over-ambitious. Far-reaching economic reconstruction ran into crucial problems of revenue and credit. State monopolies in foreign and domestic trade attempted to solve some of these problems, but merely got into a mess. A three-year plan proposed to give the country a firm industrial base with a proportion of domestic capital-formation of only about a fifth of the total thought to be required (relying on foreign aid for the rest), whereas India had allocated about 88 per cent for capital-formation from her own resources, and China as much as 96 per cent, in their respective 'first national plans'.[163]

The painful consequences of all this had begun to have their full effect by 1962, and the regime, while continuing to insist on its socialist intentions, was now putting a good deal of water in its wine. Even so, it appeared that the 'public sector' would increasingly lead the 'private sector', not only in certain basic activities, such as gold-mining and diamond-washing, but above all in the countryside, where agriculture was now moving towards fully cooperative forms of production.

Mali's position is different again. Here too the nationalist movement gathered all effective opinion behind it during the 'run up' to independence, and has since conserved this in a broad popular party, the Union Soudanaise. But Modibo Kéita and his colleagues were able (and perhaps in any case disposed) to move more cautiously than their colleagues in Guinea. They too were convinced that the 'road of free enterprise' must be, for Mali, the way of poverty and inferiority; and they were correspondingly strong adherents of the ideas of socialism and neutralism. But they were able to conserve some useful links with France for the acquisition of aid, while securing other help from other countries, both in the East and in the West. Over the past two years this land of peasants and river-fishermen has in fact moved forward with an impressive solidity. Its advance has involved the state-capitalist foundation of utilities – notably, as yet, in road, river, and rail transport – and state backing for agricultural producer cooperatives, while controls on foreign trade have gone hand in hand with the nationalization and extension of credit facilities.

In 1964 it can accordingly be said that a number of countries have gone some way towards evolving a new and viable society out of the chaos of their 'inherited situations'; while a number of others have begun to take preliminary steps in the same direction. This is a central fact of African life today, and it is one that undoubtedly bears witness to political vigour, intelligence, and courage.

The Not-Yet-Free

It scarcely needed the great summit meeting of heads of state and government at Addis Ababa, in May 1963, to emphasize another central fact of African political life – that Africa is now effectively divided between a still colonial 'south' and an emancipated 'centre and north', with the main frontier of potential conflict running along the Zambezi, or, if Southern Rhodesia should after all take the same road of peaceful change as Northern Rhodesia, along the Limpopo. What now remains to be seen is whether this frontier of political conflict must also become a frontier of war.

The 'south', indeed, is to a substantial extent already at war. Since February 1961 the Portuguese regime has been engaged in putting down a major rebellion in Angola by all the means in its power, including napalm bombings and mass executions, while continuing to assert that it will never yield an inch to African aspirations.* In so doing the Salazar dictatorship has drawn close to Dr Verwoerd's government in South Africa, to Sir Roy Welensky's Federal Government in Central Africa (dissolved at the end of 1963), and to the white-supremacy government of Mr Winston Field in Southern Rhodesia. There has come into being what their opponents have denounced as 'an unholy alliance' of these various colonial powers; and one of the early actions of this alliance, though one that failed,

* A nationalist revolt in Portuguese Guinea began in June 1962, and continues at the time of writing.

was to try to maintain the Katanga separatist regime of Moishe Tshombe in Elisabethville, in order to push 'the white frontier' a little further north.

These developments have been accompanied by a vast increase in military spending by South Africa, by the Federal Government in Central Africa (leaving Southern Rhodesia today with an air force out of all proportion to its means or needs), and, to the extent of near-bankruptcy, by the Portuguese colonial regimes in Angola and Moçambique. The South African 'defence budget' has literally soared. Offensive weapons such as the Buccaneer 'strike aircraft' – manifestly useless for purposes of internal security – have been purchased from Britain. The white population, both Afrikaner and English, has been systematically prepared for 'trouble', whether by large-scale military training, volunteer 'pistol courses' for women, or alarmist propaganda. At least one of Dr Verwoerd's Ministers has spoken of his government's need for nuclear bombs. Lately, too, there has been talk of invading Basutoland, still a British colony (though usually called a protectorate) in the middle of South Africa, and now to some extent a place of refuge for harried opponents of Dr Verwoerd's regime. A still harder hand has been laid on South-West Africa, and it has been made repeatedly clear that the regime will not voluntarily alter its policies or moderate its practices.

But if South Africa wishes to appear as the immovable object, the rest of Africa has now begun to feel itself possessed of an irresistible force. The thirty heads of state who met at Addis Ababa in May 1963 declared themselves, among other things, to be 'unanimously convinced of the imperious and urgent necessity of coordinating and intensifying their efforts to accelerate the unconditional attainment of national independence by all African territories still under foreign domination,' and pledged themselves to set about making a reality of these words.

The imminence of a clash has begun to be noticed in the outside world. Few who had studied the matter thought that it could now be long avoided. Many believed that the clash would be precipitated either by white South African pressure on

the three High Commission Territories (Basutoland, Bechuanaland, Swaziland), perhaps amounting to invasion, or by events in
and around South-West Africa.

11 Which Way Africa?

The long-range answer to the question of Africa's future will depend on pressures that are probably beyond the reach of anyone's present understanding, and are certainly beyond mine. But it appears already obvious that the crucial pressures will be those of a public opinion increasingly impatient of 'things as they are'. Such pressures seemed to be growing rapidly in 1963. 'Our leaders must realize', ran one fairly typical statement of this mounting impatience, 'that we have put them where they are not to satisfy their ambitions nor so that they can strut about in fine clothes and huge Cadillacs as ambassadors and ministers. . . . Selfish power-seekers will have to go.'[164] Thoughts like these could be heard all over the continent, though not often in quite such forthright words.

Furthermore, these growing pressures of public opinion will operate – and it is here, I hope, that this book may prove useful – within the framework of four dominant trends.

To solve the central 'problem of power' – of 'who governs whom and how' – there is first of all the trend towards the one-party state, towards concentration of all effective and even legitimate action within a single organization, within a 'liberation movement' transformed and deepened into a 'reconstruction movement'. More and more leaders have been recognizing the strength of this trend. 'As things are,' the Sardauna of Sokoto was noting of Nigeria at the end of 1962, 'there is no real reason to think that the Opposition in the Regions are ever likely to be in a position, in the foreseeable future, to form a Government. . . .'[165]

On the same point, a little earlier, the Minister of the Interior of Mali, Madéira Kéita, was arguing that full recognition of the reality of this situation – acceptance, that is, of a single unified party of 'government and opposition' – made for 'greater honesty, great disinterestedness, greater devotion' among politicians, and all the more because in Africa today 'you cannot remain a leader for very long unless you are really effective'.[166] Public opinion, in other words, cannot be ignored; and public opinion demands progress.

To solve the problem of development – of economic and social progress – there is the trend towards state capitalism, and, among the committed countries, its deliberate extension in the direction of socialism. Thirdly, to the problem of the cold war and its conflict of loyalties, the general answer is a more or less emphatic neutralism. And, last but not least, in response to the problem of inter-African relations there is the effort to secure continental unity of policy, action, and institutions.

It is early in the day to be sure of what the atmosphere, the mood and style of independent African civilization, will be like. On the whole, though, it appears that this atmosphere will not be narrowly nationalist, intolerant, or bellicose. There are, true enough, signs to the contrary. White racism has sometimes tended, most obviously in South Africa, to produce its African counterpart. But even here the signs are far from clear. Quite often they seem to owe less to reality than to European imagination. The Malawi Congress party in Nyasaland, it will be remembered, was accused of conspiring to massacre Europeans; but the charge was then shown by a British judicial inquiry to be groundless.[167] The following extract from a British newspaper suggests that accusations of chauvinism and violence should be received with caution.

During the recent election campaign in Nyasaland [that of 1961] a fierce campaign was waged by a section of the Press of this country and by a group of Tory M.P.s against Dr Banda's Malawi Party, alleging that it was victimizing its opponents by burning down their homes. At one stage the campaign reached the point where Sir Roy Welensky [then Federal Prime Minister in Central Africa] canvassed the idea of putting off the elections because of this alleged victimization.

The worst incident was said to have occurred at Mbobo, where three houses were destroyed, including that of Mr Chijalo, the local chairman of Sir Roy Welensky's United Federal Party. At the time two of Dr Banda's supporters were convicted; one youth was given twelve strokes with a cane. Last week Mr Chijalo was himself convicted for conspiring to defeat justice and sentenced to eighteen months' imprisonment. He has also been charged with two other members of the United Federal Party with burning down their own houses. It is a pity that these events have not been given equal prominence in those papers which gave so much prominence to the allegations against Malawi at the time. The boy who was whipped after being wrongfully convicted has been paid £10 as compensation.[168]

Europeans, of course, find many occasions for irritation – some petty and spiteful – in independent Africa. I have already quoted the case of the twenty-nine Europeans who were turned out of a Tanganyika hotel for failing to recognize President Touré of Guinea. But all in all it is hard to understand how a newspaper like the *Guardian* can bring itself to write that 'Africa has not yet had time to throw up the new generation of leaders who will see Africa as something more edifying than a racial battleground'.[169] For the weight of evidence comes out as remarkably at odds with any such conclusion. Victorious Algerians have not massacred Frenchmen; independent West Africans have not ceased to employ large numbers of whites; emancipated East Africans have not turned their backs on European friendship. Even a 'hard-core detainee' of the 'Mau Mau' emergency in Kenya, J. M. Kariuki, can write after seven years of detention in fourteen camps and much beating and harsh treatment that 'there will be no spirit of revenge to destroy our new Kenya'; while Dr Margery Perham adds in her foreword to his book that she found Kariuki possessed of 'a healing desire for reconciliation with those Europeans or Africans who had ill-treated him'.[170] The general temper of Africa today appears to be resiliently tolerant and healthy.

There are none the less plenty of practical dangers ahead. The existence of the one-party state is obviously in itself no guarantee of successful reconstruction. Where it rests on wide democratic foundations, as it does in some countries, it can offer a clear way forward to social and economic transformation, for it enables a government to act boldly, consistently, and with a maximum of public support. But failure to deliver the goods – failure, that is, to take the right basic decisions, or, what again amounts to the same thing, failure to adopt and evolve a constructive ideology as a guide to policy and action – must soon bring conflicts of interest and opinion. Unless creatively resolved, these conflicts must either inhibit the government from action – and thereby, in stopping the process of expansive change, deepen the conflicts themselves – or else drive the 'ruling circles' to group measures of self-defence. And such measures, as we all know by this time, generally mean an end to democracy. Thus it is not the one-party system which threatens dictatorship in Africa, but failure to use this system to achieve democratic social change. The danger of 'Bonapartism' comes from standing still, not from going forward.

That this is really so may be seen by looking at the countries which maintain more than one party. Here again the measure of effective democracy will clearly be decided by the measure of effective change towards that new society which the East Africa Royal Commission, among others, so strongly declared was now necessary. Given the driving desire for a better and larger life that exists in nearly all parts of Africa today, no quantity of parties or complexity of parliamentary rules will be able to withstand the shattering impact of a failure to get on with the job of reconstruction. What may be expected to happen then is that one or other group will seize power – as in the different but none the less highly relevant case of Latin America – and hold it until ousted, more or less violently, by another group. And if the group which holds power should be firmly embedded in the *status quo* – as was the True Whig Party in Liberia through decades of stagnant rule in the past – then the country in question will not only stand still, but will fall into still deeper poverty and helplessness.

One may go further. The 'state capitalist' solution is likewise in itself no guarantee of successful development. It may be used, after all, merely to promote the interests of a favoured economic minority. By and large, this was what happened with state capitalism in Mussolini's Italy, where large-scale nationalization of certain basic industries was made to work in favour of a much more profitable 'private sector'. A development towards that kind of dictatorship is clearly possible in Egypt today, not to mention other countries, and will remain so until the regime can democratize itself. A large amount of state capitalism is manifestly inevitable in Africa: its success, however, will depend on the extent to which its future growth is made to serve nation-wide as distinct from minority interests. The test of health, in short, will be the degree in which the 'private sector' – inevitably, as things are, a weak native capitalism allied with foreign private investment – is dominated by the 'public sector' under government control.

It is in this direction that one should look for guidance on the future. Compared with basic decisions on the *use* of power, the panoply of many-partied parliaments will have no more influence in favour of expansive democracy, than the various manifestations of 'personality cults' around charismatic leaders will have against it. The one no more guarantees democracy – ensures outward-growing forms of social life – than the other threatens it. The deciding factor in Ghana, for instance, is not that certain boot-lickers should insist that children chant slogans like 'Nkrumah never dies, Nkrumah does no wrong' – the children don't believe it anyway – but the extent to which President Nkrumah's government is solving the post-colonial crisis. The deciding factor in Nigeria, similarly, lies not in any individual corruption or irresponsibility such as the Coker Commission revealed, but in the capacity of Nigerian politics to build and operate a unified and enlightened movement of social reconstruction.

Where 'personality cults' really count for evil, it will be found, the main damage has already occurred. For it is not the cult which makes the dictator, but the dictator who makes the cult. Once a dictator were to seize power in independent Africa, no doubt he would quickly build as noxious a cult as anywhere else. And here, once again, the countries which give cause for alarm of this kind are those where social and political life stands still,* not those where it changes. All that countries of the latter type are engaged in doing, in terms of 'personal homage', is to bury the colonial past. Thus the Dar-es-Salaam city council was lately reported to have suggested changing no fewer than eighty-five street names: '. . . out go such [names] as Queen's Close, Queen's Drive, Royal Close . . . and in come such

* Morocco in late 1963 offered a startlingly relevant example.

178

[names] as Kenyatta Drive, Kimathi Road, Kaunda Drive, Banda Close, Touré Drive, Ghana Avenue ....'[171] But can anyone seriously think that Tanganyika is labouring under the burden of a 'personality cult'?

The crucial indicator, then, lies in the degree to which the problem of power, posed both by the withdrawal of colonial rule and by the fact of social and economic crisis, gets itself solved in a popular-democratic as distinct from a merely parliamentary-democratic or party-bureaucratic sense.

The truth of this seems to emerge from every *real* problem in Africa today. How is it going to be possible, for example, to spend money successfully on agricultural development – the necessary ground for every advance in this continent now – unless farmers and peasants can be carried into willing and intelligent participation? The mere distribution of tractors, fertilizers, instructors, and the like will accomplish little but waste and disillusion unless these new instruments are used to refashion the traditional system, and they cannot be so used without their *active* acceptance by country folk who are still embedded in traditional ways of thought. Such active acceptance of the need for far-reaching change depends on wedding the cause of political independence to the cause of social and economic reconstruction. And the same may be said of the multiplication of schools and universities, or the founding of new industries. Their fruitfulness will depend on the creation of a political climate which is keyed to expansion – in Africa today, to rapid and deliberate social change; and this in turn can only be the product of a massive 'activation' of democracy. But that will be, as it always is, very different from a mere activity of parliaments or party bosses.

There is a useful analogy in the history of Russia. African political independence on its own can no more emancipate the vast majority of Africans than the simple ending of serfdom could emancipate the vast majority of Russians. Professor Carr has pointed out that Tsar Alexander's emancipation of 1861 'did not, in any absolute sense, emancipate the peasant. Where no alternative employment and no avenue of escape was available, it could not materially raise the level of the peasantry as a whole. It ushered in a period of growing population and chronic

hunger in the Russian countryside, culminating in the cata-
strophic famine of 1891.'[172] What was needed was a new social
and economic framework. And this was provided for the
Russian peasant by the Communist revolution. It remains to be
seen how it will be provided for the African peasant: what seems
beyond doubt is that a new framework *must* be provided if
Africa is to escape from poverty and stagnation.

It is especially in this context that the concept of 'neo-
colonialism' is now increasingly used by African leaders and
politicians. Their point of departure is not obscure. For if it
appears to them that the conservative fears and hostility of the
Western world have often helped to guarantee the revolutionary
nature of Russian (and Chinese) solutions, it also appears to
them that the qualified readiness of the Western world to aid
Africa may here produce the contrary effect – may slow down
or even stop the search for that new social framework without
which, as more and more Africans believe, their political
initiatives must prove futile.

It is not difficult to see why this danger appears to loom so
large. Viewed in a detached and historical perspective, the
broad alternative emerges: *either* a prolongation of the *status quo*
– however disguised by the trappings of political sovereignty –
or a movement into a radically different situation. Radically
different of necessity: for the weakness of all independent
African economies today means that the 'free enterprise'
solution – the positive extension of the *status quo* – cannot be
effective in the foreseeable future. That is why so many politically conscious Africans will be found to listen with attention
whenever ex-colonial countries claim to have 'by-passed the
capitalist stage'. When the head of the United Nations Technical
Assistance Board, Mr David Owen, said in New York recently
that the People's Republic of Mongolia had 'moved from
feudalism to socialism, by-passing the capitalist stage',[173] he
was saying something which will have seemed highly relevant
to Africa, not because Africans would want to adopt the same
methods (though they might want to adopt some of them)
but because this offered a practical example of how to recon-
struct a colonial society. It is the same angle of interest that
regularly sends African visitors in the Soviet Union to the

ex-colonial lands of Central Asia. They want to see if these countries have been freed from their dusty and subservient past, and, if they have, then how. This is what neutralist-minded Africans – and there are few others of much influence now – mean by 'freedom to choose'. Quite apart from any question of communism, which indeed seems very remote from the reality of Africa today, any suggestion that Western aid is tied to hopes of prolonging the *status quo* is likely to meet with growing resentment. By the same token, of course, it is accepted that Western aid which is *not* so tied will enormously help in the task of transition, and great efforts are being made to secure it.

The conclusion is that there can be no expansion of democracy in Africa without radical structural change, and that, in the absence of this or the determined attempt to get it, we may shortly witness a contrary movement into authoritarian types of rule. But this conclusion is in turn conditioned by another line of thought, by another central question. Can there be radical social reconstruction within an Africa divided into a multitude of states, none of which has equalled (Ghana perhaps apart) the average income for each inhabitant of so poor a European country as Portugal?

This question is also much discussed. Nobody has said yes to it yet; but quite a few have said no. Nkrumah put the latter view to the Addis conference in dramatic terms. There was, he declared, no time to waste, 'for we must unite or perish ...'. His emphasis there was on the danger of neo-colonialism in the sense noted above: 'No African state is large or powerful enough to stand on its own against the unbridled imperialist exploitation of her men and resources and the growing complexities of the modern world.' Over and beyond that particular argument, however, he also noted that 'frontier disputes, economic difficulties, political disagreements ... [are hanging] like a Sword of Damocles over the Independent African States ...'; and even a glance round the bristling field of inter-African stress and strain will quickly confirm that he is right. Others have pressed the same line of thought. Among them are the leaders of East and Central Africa whose main intention has been to follow the separate independence of their countries by federation into a single state. The same note is repeatedly struck, though in face of greater obstacles, by leading politicians in North Africa as well. The stable states in Africa are the changing states.

Having said this, no doubt, one has still not said very much. The actual solutions largely remain to be found and made, or, if found here and there, to prove themselves in practice. Meanwhile, in this complex and continental struggle for a new society, there will be many upheavals among regimes and governments – as with Congo-Brazzaville and Dahomey in 1963 – which so far represent little more, in practice, than provisional rearrangements of the colonial situation. All this will form a sequel that cannot yet be written. But what that sequel will reveal, I suggest, is not only that Africans will make their own particular contributions to the sum of political wisdom and economic welfare – for this they will obviously do – but that the decisive African societies of the future (and sooner, perhaps, than we expect) will marry and merge their old traditions of equality with modern ideas of equality; and will build a new civilization in this continent that will add, as one of their poets has foretold, 'a fresh colour to the rainbow'.

Meanwhile, the battle is everywhere engaged. The 1950s presided over the struggle for political emancipation. The 1960s and maybe the 1970s will preside over an even greater struggle for the fruits of political emancipation – for that new and unified society without which the peoples of Africa cannot independently survive or prosper.

On the Record
The Charter of Unity

Addis Ababa, 25 May 1963

We, the Heads of African States and Governments assembled in the city of Addis Ababa, Ethiopia;

CONVINCED that it is the inalienable right of all people to control their own destiny;

CONSCIOUS of the fact that freedom, equality, justice, and dignity are essential objectives for the achievement of the legitimate aspirations of the African peoples;

CONSCIOUS of our responsibility to harness the natural and human resources of our continent for the total advancement of our peoples in spheres of human endeavour;

INSPIRED by a common determination to strengthen understanding and cooperation among our states in response to the aspirations of our peoples for brotherhood and solidarity, in a large unity transcending ethnic and national differences;

CONVINCED that, in order to translate this determination into a dynamic force in the cause of human progress, conditions for peace and security must be established and maintained;

DETERMINED to safeguard and consolidate the hard-won independence as well as the sovereignty and territorial integrity of our states, and to fight against neo-colonialism in all its forms;

DEDICATED to the general progress of Africa;

PERSUADED that the Charter of the United Nations and the Universal Declaration of Human Rights, to the principles of which we reaffirm our adherence, provide a solid foundation for peaceful and positive cooperation among states;

DESIROUS that all African states should henceforth unite so that the welfare and well-being of their peoples can be assured;

RESOLVED to reinforce the links between our states by establishing and strengthening common institutions;

HAVE agreed to the present Charter.

Establishment

Article I. (1) The High Contracting Parties do by the present Charter establish an organization to be known as the 'Organization of African Unity'.

(2) The organization shall include the continental African states, Madagascar, and all the islands surrounding Africa.

Purposes

Article II. (1) The organization shall have the following purposes: (a) to promote the unity and solidarity of the African states; (b) to coordinate and intensify their cooperation and efforts to achieve a better life for the peoples of Africa; (c) to defend their sovereignty, their territorial integrity, and independence; (d) to eradicate all forms of colonialism from Africa; and (e) to promote international cooperation, having due regard to the Charter of the United Nations and the Universal Declaration of Human Rights.

(2) To these ends, the member states shall coordinate and harmonize their general policies, especially in the following fields: (a) political and diplomatic cooperation; (b) economic cooperation, including transport and communications; (c) educational and cultural cooperation; (d) health, sanitation, and nutritional cooperation; (e) scientific and technical cooperation; and (f) cooperation for defence and security.

Principles

Article III. The member states, in pursuit of the purposes stated in Article II, solemnly affirm and declare their adherence to the following principles:

(1) the sovereign equality of all member states;

(2) non-interference in the internal affairs of states;

(3) respect for the sovereignty and territorial integrity of each member state and for its inalienable right to independent existence;

(4) peaceful settlement of disputes, by negotiation, mediation, conciliation, or arbitration;

(5) unreserved condemnation, in all its forms, of political assassination as well as of subversive activities on the part of neighbouring states or any other states;

(6) absolute dedication to the total emancipation of the African territories which are still dependent;

(7) affirmation of a policy of non-alignment with regard to all blocs.

Membership

Article IV. Each independent sovereign African state shall be entitled to become a member of the organization.

Rights and Duties of Member States

Article V. All member states shall enjoy equal rights and have equal duties.

Article VI. The member states pledge themselves to observe scrupulously the principles enumerated in Article III of the present Charter.

Institutions

Article VII. The organization shall accomplish its purposes through the following principal institutions:

(1) the Assembly of Heads of State and Government;

(2) the Council of Ministers;

(3) the General Secretariat;

(4) the Commission of Mediation, Conciliation, and Arbitration.

The Assembly of Heads of State and Government

Article VIII. The Assembly of Heads of State and Government shall be the supreme organ of the organization. It shall, subject to the provisions of this Charter, discuss matters of common concern to Africa with a view to coordinating and harmonizing the general policy of the organization. It may in addition review the structure, functions, and acts of all the organs and any specialized agencies which may be created in accordance with the present Charter.

Article IX. The Assembly shall be composed of the Heads of State, Government, or their duly accredited representatives, and it shall meet at least *once a year*. At the request of any member state, and approval by the majority of the member states, the Assembly shall meet in extraordinary session.

Article X. (1) Each member state shall have one vote.

(2) All resolutions shall be determined by a two-thirds majority of the members of the organization.

(3) Questions of procedure shall require a simple majority. Whether or not a question is one of procedure shall be determined by a simple majority of all member states of the organization.

(4) Two-thirds of the total membership of the organization shall form a quorum at any meeting of the Assembly.

Article XI. The Assembly shall have the power to determine its own rules of procedure.

The Council of Ministers

Article XII. The Council of Ministers shall consist of Foreign Ministers or such other Ministers as are designated by the Governments of member states.

The Council of Ministers shall meet at least twice a year. When requested by any member state and approved by two-thirds of all member states, it shall meet in extraordinary session.

Article XIII. The Council of Ministers shall be responsible to the Assembly of Heads of State and Government. It shall be entrusted with the responsibility of preparing conferences of the Assembly.

It shall take cognizance of any matter referred to it by the Assembly. It shall be entrusted with the implementation of the decisions of the Assembly of Heads of State and Government. It shall coordinate inter-African cooperation in accordance with the instructions of the Assembly and in conformity with Article II (2) of the present Charter.

Article XIV. (1) Each member state shall have one vote.

(2) All resolutions shall be determined by a simple majority of the Council of Ministers.

(3) Two-thirds of the total membership of the Council shall form a quorum for any meeting of the Council.

Article XV. The Council shall have the power to determine its own rule of procedure.

General Secretariat

Article XVI. There shall be an Administrative Secretary-

General of the organization, who shall be appointed by the Assembly of Heads of State and Government, on the recommendation of the Council of Ministers. The Administrative Secretary-General shall direct the affairs of the Secretariat.

Article XVII. There shall be one or more Assistant Secretaries-General of the organization, who shall be appointed by the Assembly of Heads of State and Government.

Article XVIII. The functions and conditions of service of the Secretary-General, of the Assistant Secretaries-General, and of other employees of the Secretariat shall be governed by the provisions of this Charter and the regulations approved by the Assembly of Heads of State and Government.

(1) In the performance of their duties the Administrative Secretary-General and the staff shall not seek or receive instructions from any government or from any other authority external to the organization. They shall refrain from any action which might reflect on their position as international officials responsible only to the organization.

(2) Each member of the organization undertakes to respect the exclusive character of the responsibilities of the Administrative Secretary-General and the staff and not to seek to influence them in the discharge of their responsibilities.

Commission of Mediation, Conciliation, and Arbitration

Article XIX. Member states pledge to settle all disputes among themselves by peaceful means and, to this end, decide to establish a Commission of Mediation, Conciliation, and Arbitration, the composition of which and the condition of service shall be defined by a separate protocol to be approved by the Assembly of Heads of State and Government.

Specialized Commissions

Article XX. The Assembly shall establish such Specialized Commissions as it may deem necessary, including the following:

(1) Economic and Social Commission;
(2) Educational and Cultural Commission;
(3) Health, Sanitation, and Nutrition Commission;
(4) Defence Commission;
(5) Scientific, Technical, and Research Commission.

Article XXI. Each Specialized Commission referred to in Article XX shall be composed of the Ministers concerned or other Ministers or Plenipotentiaries designated by the Governments of the member states.

Article XXII. The functions of the Specialized Commissions shall be carried out in accordance with the provisions of the present Charter and of the regulations approved by the Council of Ministers.

The Budget

Article XXIII. The budget of the organization prepared by the Administrative Secretary-General shall be approved by the Council of Ministers. The budget shall be provided by contributions from member states in accordance with the scale of assessment of the United Nations; provided, however, that no member state shall be assessed an amount exceeding twenty per cent of the yearly regular budget of the organization. The member states agree to pay their respective contributions regularly.

Signature and Ratification of Charter

Article XXIV. This Charter shall be open for signature to all independent sovereign African states and shall be ratified by the signatory states in accordance with their respective constitutional processes.

The original instrument, done, if possible, in African languages, in English and French, all texts being equally authentic, shall be deposited with the Government of Ethiopia, which shall transmit certified copies thereof to all independent sovereign African states.

Instruments of ratification shall be deposited with the Government of Ethiopia, which shall notify all signatories of each such deposit.

Entry into Force

Article XXV. This Charter shall enter into force immediately upon receipt by the Government of Ethiopia of the instruments of ratification from two-thirds of the signatory states.

Registration of the Charter

Article XXVI. This Charter shall, after due ratification, be registered with the Secretariat of the United Nations through the Government of Ethiopia in conformity with Article 102 of the Charter of the United Nations.

Interpretation of the Charter

Article XXVII. (1) Any question which may arise concerning the interpretation of this Charter shall be decided by a vote of two-thirds of the Assembly of Heads of State and Government of the organizations.

Adhesion and Accession

Article XXVIII. (1) Any independent sovereign African State may at any time notify the Administrative Secretary-General of its intention to adhere or accede to this Charter.

(2) The Administrative Secretary-General shall, on receipt of such notification, communicate a copy of it to all the member states. Admission shall be decided by a simple majority of member states. The decision of each member state shall be transmitted to the Administrative Secretary-General, who shall, upon receipt of the required number of votes, communicate the decision to the state concerned.

Miscellaneous

Article XXIX. The working languages of the organization and all its institutions shall be, if possible, African languages, English, and French.

Article XXX. The Administrative Secretary-General may accept on behalf of the organization gifts, bequests, and other donations made to the organization, provided that this is approved by the Council of Ministers.

Article XXXI. The Council of Ministers shall decide on the privileges and immunities to be accorded to the personnel of the Secretariat in the respective territories of the member states.

Cessation of Membership

Article XXXII. Any state which desires to renounce its membership shall forward a written notification to the Adminis-

trative Secretary-General. At the end of one year from the date
of such notification, if not withdrawn, the Charter shall cease to
apply with respect to the renouncing state, which shall thereby
cease to belong to the organization.

Amendment to the Charter

Article XXXIII. This Charter may be amended or revised if
any member state makes a written request to the Administrative
Secretary-General to that effect, provided, however, that the
proposed amendment is not submitted to the Assembly for consideration until all the member states have been duly notified of
it and a period of one year has elapsed. Such an amendment shall
not be effective unless approved by at least two-thirds of all the
member states.

In faith, whereof, We, the Heads of African State and
Government, have signed this Charter.

Done in the City of Addis Ababa, Ethiopia, this 25th day of
May, 1963.

1. Algeria: Premier Ahmed Ben Bella
2. Burundi: King Mwambutsa
3. Cameroon: President Ahmadou Ahidjo
4. Central African Republic: President David Dacko
5. Chad: President François Tombalbaye
6. Congo-Brazzaville: President Fulbert Youlou
7. Congo-Leopoldville: President Joseph Kasavubu
8. Dahomey: President Hubert Maga
9. Ethiopia: Emperor Haile Selassie I
10. Gabon: President Leon M'Ba
11. Ghana: President Kwame Nkrumah
12. Guinea: President Sékou Touré
13. Ivory Coast: President Félix Houphouët-Boigny
14. Liberia: President William V. S. Tubman
15. Libya: King Idris I
16. Malagasy Republic: President Philibert Tsiranana
17. Mali: President Modibo Kéita
18. Mauritania: President Makhtar Ould Daddah
19. Niger: President Hamani Diori
20. Nigeria: Prime Minister Alhaji Sir Abubakar Tafawa
   Balewa

21. Ruanda: Foreign Minister Callixte Habamenshi for President Grégoire Kayibanda
22. Senegal: President Leopold Sédar Senghor
23. Sierra Leone: Prime Minister Sir Milton Margai
24. Somali Republic: President Abdullah Osman
25. Sudan: President Ibrahim Abboud
26. Tanganyika: President Julius Nyerere
27. Tunisia: President Habib Bourguiba
28. Uganda: Prime Minister Milton Obote
29. United Arab Republic: President Gamal Abdul Nasser
30. Upper Volta: President Maurice Yaméogo

Not Present:

1. Morocco: King Hassan II
2. Togo: President Nicolas Grunitzky

THE RESOLUTIONS

I. *Decolonization*

The Summit Conference of Independent African States meeting in Addis Ababa, Ethiopia, from 22 May to 25 May 1963; *having considered* all aspects of the questions of decolonization; *unanimously convinced* of the imperious and urgent necessity of coordinating and intensifying their efforts to accelerate the unconditional attainment of national independence by all African territories still under foreign domination; *reaffirming* that it is the duty of all African independent states to support dependent people in Africa in their struggle for freedom and independence; *noting* with deep concern that most of the remaining dependent territories in Africa are dominated by foreign settlers; *convinced* that the colonial powers by their forcible imposition of the settlers to control the governments and administration of those territories are thus establishing colonial bases in the heart of Africa; *have agreed* unanimously to concert and coordinate their efforts and action in this field, and to this end have decided on the following measures:

(1) *Declares* that the forcible imposition by the colonial powers of the settlers to control the governments and administration of the dependent territories is a flagrant violation of the inalienable rights of the legitimate inhabitants of the territories concerned;

(2) *Invites* the colonial powers to take the necessary measures for the immediate application of the declaration on the granting of independence to colonial countries and peoples by insisting on the fact that their determination to maintain colonies or semi-colonies in Africa constitutes a menace to the peace of the continent;

(3) *Invites* further the colonial powers, particularly the United Kingdom with regard to Southern Rhodesia, not to transfer the powers and attributes of sovereignty to foreign minority governments imposed on African peoples by the use of force and under cover of racial legislation. A transfer of this kind would amount to a violation of the provisions of United Nations resolution 1514 on independence;

(4) *Reaffirms* its support of African nationalists of Southern Rhodesia and solemnly declares that if power in Southern Rhodesia were to be usurped by a racial white minority government, the states members of the Conference would lend their effective moral and practical support to any legitimate measures which the African nationalist leaders may devise for the purpose of recovering such power and restoring it to the African majority. The Conference undertakes henceforth to concert the efforts of its members to take such measures as the situation demands against any state according to such recognition;

(5) *Reaffirms* that the territory of South-West Africa is an African territory under international mandate and that any attempt by the Republic of South Africa to annex it would be regarded as an act of aggression; *Reaffirms* also its determination to render all necessary support to the second phase of the South-West Africa case before the International Court of Justice; *Reaffirms*, further, the inalienable right of the people of South-West Africa to self-determination and independence;

(6) *Intervenes* expressly with the great powers so that they cease without exception to lend directly or indirectly any support or assistance to all those colonialist governments which might use such assistance to suppress African national liberation movements, particularly the Portuguese Government, which is conducting a real war of genocide in Africa. *Informs* the allies of colonial powers that they must choose between their friendship

for the African peoples and their support of powers that oppress African peoples;

(7) *Sends* a delegation of Ministers of Foreign Affairs to speak on behalf of all African states at the meeting of the Security Council which will be called to examine the report of the United Nations Committee of 26 on the situation in African territories under Portuguese domination;

(8) *Demands* the breaking off of diplomatic and consular relations between all African states and the Governments of Portugal and South Africa so long as they persist in their present attitude towards decolonization;

(9) *Asks for an effective boycott* of the foreign trade of Portugal and South Africa by (a) prohibiting the import of goods from those two countries; (b) closing African ports and airports to their ships and planes; (c) forbidding the planes of those two countries to overfly the territories of all African states;

(10) *Earnestly invites* all national liberation movements to coordinate their efforts by establishing common action fronts wherever necessary so as to strengthen the effectiveness of their struggle and the rational use of the concerted assistance given them;

(11) *Establishes* a coordinating committee consisting of Ethiopia, Algeria, Uganda, U.A.R., Tanganyika, Congo-Leopoldville, Guinea, Senegal, and Nigeria, with headquarters in Dar-es-Salaam, responsible for harmonizing the assistance from African states and for managing the special fund to be set up for that purpose;

(12) *Establishes* a special fund to be contributed by member states with the deadline (15 July) to supply the necessary practical and financial aid to the various African national liberation movements;

(13) *Appoints* the day of 25 May 1963, as African Liberation Day and will organize popular demonstrations on that day to disseminate the recommendations of the Heads of State Conference and to collect sums, over and above the national contributions, for the special fund;

(14) *Receives*, on the territories of independent African states, nationalists from liberation movements in order to give them

training in all sectors, and afford young people all the assistance they need for their education and vocational training;

(15) *Promotes*, in each state, the establishment of a body of volunteers in various fields, with a view to providing the various African national liberation movements with the assistance they need in the various sectors;

(16) *Fixes* a deadline for the accession of all African territories to independence.

II. *Apartheid and Racial Discrimination*

The Summit Conference of Independent African States, *having considered* all aspects of the questions of apartheid and racial discrimination; *unanimously convinced* of the imperious and urgent necessity of coordinating and intensifying their efforts to put an end to the South African Government's criminal policy of apartheid and wipe out racial discrimination in all its forms; *have agreed* unanimously to concert and coordinate their efforts and action in this field, and to this end have decided on the following measures:

(1) Creation of a fund for concerted financial assistance to the anti-apartheid movement in South Africa.

(2) Effective assistance of every kind to anti-apartheid movements in South Africa to help them carry out their struggle for freedom efficiently.

(3) The immediate release of Mr Mandela, Mr Sobukwe, and all other political prisoners in South Africa.

(4) Granting of scholarships, educational facilities, and possibilities of employment in African government service to refugees from South Africa.

(5) Supporting the recommendations presented to the Security Council and the General Assembly by the Special Committee of the United Nations on the apartheid policies of the South African Government.

(6) Despatch of a delegation of Foreign Ministers to inform the Security Council of the explosive situation existing in South Africa.

(7) Coordination of concrete measures of sanction against the Government of South Africa.

(8) Appeal to all states, and more particularly to those which have traditional relations and cooperate with the Government of South Africa, strictly to apply U.N. resolution 1761 of 6 November 1962, concerning apartheid.

(9) Appeal to all governments who still have diplomatic, consular, and economic relations with the Government of South Africa to break off those relations and to cease any other form of encouragement for the policy of apartheid.

(10) Stress the great responsibility incurred by the colonial authorities of territories neighbouring of South Africa for the pursuit of the policy of apartheid.

(11) Condemnation of racial discrimination in all its forms in Africa and all over the world.

(12) Expression of the deep concern aroused in all African peoples and governments by the measures of racial discrimination taken against communities of African origin living outside the continent and particularly in the United States of America. Expression of appreciation for the efforts of the Federal Government of the United States of America to put an end to these intolerable malpractices which are likely seriously to deteriorate relations between the African peoples and governments on the one hand and the people and government of the United States of America on the other.

III. *Africa, Non-Alignment, and the United Nations*

The Summit Conference, *believing* that the United Nations is an important instrument for the maintenance of peace and security among nations and for the promotion of the economic and social advancement of all peoples; *reiterating* its desire to strengthen and support the United Nations; *noting* with regret that Africa as a region is not equitably represented in the principal organs of the United Nations; *convinced* of the need for closer cooperation and coordination among the African states members of the United Nations:

(1) *Reaffirms* its dedication to the purposes and principles of the United Nations Charter, and its acceptance of all obligations contained in the Charter, including financial obligations;

(2) *Insists* that Africa as a geographical region should have

195

equitable representation in the principal organs of the United Nations, particularly the Security Council and the Economic and Social Council and its Specialized Agencies;

(3) *Invites* African governments to instruct their representatives in the United Nations to take all possible steps to achieve a more equitable representation of the African region;

(4) *Further invites* African governments to instruct their representatives in the United Nations, without prejudice to their membership in and collaboration with the African-Asian group, to constitute a more effective African Group to bring about closer cooperation and better coordination in matters of common concern.

IV. *General Disarmament*

The Summit Conference, *having considered* all aspects of the question of general disarmament; *unanimously convinced* of the imperious and urgent necessity of coordinating and intensifying their efforts to contribute to the achievement of a realistic disarmament programme through the signing, by all states concerned, of a Treaty on general and complete disarmament under strict and effective international control; *have agreed* unanimously to concert and coordinate their efforts and action in these various fields, and to this end have decided on the following measures:

(1) To declare and accept Africa as a denuclearized zone, the banning of nuclear and thermonuclear tests; the peaceful use of nuclear energy and the banning of the manufacture of nuclear weapons.

(2) The destruction of existing nuclear weapons.

(3) The removal of military bases from Africa and disentanglement of African countries from military pacts with foreign powers.

(4) To appeal to the great powers to: (a) reduce conventional weapons; (b) put an end to the arms race; and (c) sign a general and complete disarmament agreement under strict and effective international control.

(5) To appeal to the great powers, in particular to the Soviet Union and the United States of America, to use their best endeavours to secure the objectives stated above.

(6) To undertake to bring about by means of negotiation the

end of military occupation in the African continent, the elimination of military bases and nuclear tests which constitute an essential element of African independence and unity.

V. *Economic Problems*

The Summit Conference, *concerned* with the active share of the developing countries in world trade and at the persistent deterioration of the terms of trade in these external commercial relationships; *conscious* of the fact that owing to its extreme dependence on the export of primary products, Africa and Madagascar more than any other developing region are adversely affected by persistent deteriorations in export earnings; *convinced* of the necessity for concerted action by the African countries and Madagascar in order to ensure a much more remunerative price from the sale of their primary products; *mindful* of the need to eliminate the barriers to trade between the African states and thereby to strengthen their economies; *considering* that economic development, including the expansion of trade on the basis of fair and remunerative prices, should tend to eliminate the need for external economic aid, and that such external economic aid should be unconditional and should not prejudice the independence of African states; *considering* the imperative necessity for African countries to pool their resources and harmonize their activities in the economic field; *aware of* the necessity for the joint utilization of river basin resources, the study of the use of Saharan zones, the coordination of means of transport and communication systems, and the provision of research facilities, all of which serve to stimulate economic growth and expansion of trade, both regionally and inter-regionally; *convinced* that the acceleration of the rate of economic and social development of the various African countries lies in the industrialization of these countries and the diversification of their production; *considering* the serious problems arising from the great shortage of trained and skilled personnel, the lack of qualified staff, scarce capital resources, grossly inadequate infra-structure, limited outlets for industrial products and the far too inadequate participation of Africans in the economic construction of their countries; *desiring* to explore the effects of regional economic groupings of the African economy; *noting* with satisfaction that the Executive

Secretary of the Economic Commission for Africa has decided to convene a Conference of African Ministers of Finance, to be held in Khartoum (Sudan) in July 1963, with a view to setting up an African Development Bank; *resolves to*:

(1) Appoint a preparatory economic committee to study, in collaboration with governments and in consultation with the Economic Commission for Africa, *inter alia*, the following questions and submit their findings to member states: (a) the possibility of establishing a free trade area between the various African countries; (b) the establishment of a common external tariff to protect the emergent industries and the setting up of a raw material price stabilization fund; (c) the restructuralization of international trade; (d) means for developing trade between African countries by the organization of and participation in African trade fairs and exhibitions and by the granting of transport and transit facilities; (e) the coordination of means of transport and the establishment of road, air, and maritime companies; (f) the establishment of an African Payments and Clearing Union; (g) a progressive freeing of national currencies from all non-technical external attachments and the establishment of a Pan-African monetary zone; (h) ways and means of effecting the harmonization of existing and future national development plans;

(2) Invite the Economic Commission for Africa to request their Executive Secretary to give the Commission of Experts all the necessary support and assistance which it may require in the fulfilment of its assignment;

(3) Welcome the forthcoming Conference of African Ministers of Finance and give the respective Ministers of Finance instructions to take the necessary measures for the rapid establishment of the African Development Bank;

(4) The Summit Conference of Independent African States note with satisfaction the progress achieved by the Economic Commission for Africa in establishing the Dakar Institute of Economic Development and Planning and affirm their profound interest in that Institute and their intention of giving it appropriate financial and other support;

(5) Welcome the forthcoming World Conference on Trade and Development which is to examine international trade

problems in relation to the economic development of emerging countries;

(6) *Urge* all states concerned to conduct negotiations, in concert, with a view to obtaining from the consumer countries real price stabilization and guaranteed outlets on the world market so that the developing countries may derive considerably greater revenue from international trade.

VI. *The future of the CCTA*

The Summit Conference, *considering* that at the last CCTA session in Dar-es-Salaam in January to February 1963, the final adoption of the new CCTA convention was deferred until the Heads of African States had had an opportunity to consider and direct on the role of the CCTA within the overall context of Pan-African cooperation; *and in view* of the fact that Article 23 of this new convention lays down as follows: 'Pending the signature and the ratification of this convention as provided in Article 16, the Parties having initialled this convention agree to apply it provisionally as if it had entered into force as from the date of initialling, subject to any decision which may be taken by the Heads of African States at the Conference at Addis Ababa or at any subsequent conference on the role of the CCTA within the overall context of Pan-African cooperation'; decides to reconsider its role in order to bring it eventually within the scope of the organization of African states which will have, as one of its arms, an organ for technical, scientific, and cultural cooperation.

References

1 *Fighting Talk*, Johannesburg, August 1961.
2 Mr Henry Hopkinson when Minister of State at the Colonial Office, quoted in Patrick Keatley: *The Politics of Partnership*, Penguin African Library, London, 1963, p. 389.
3 Thomas Hodgkin in *African Political Parties*, London, 1961, lists 239 leading parties, congresses, and movements.
4 Roland Oliver and J. D. Fage, *A Short History of Africa*, Penguin African Library, London, 1962, p. 49.
5 Jean Leclant, 'Égypte pharaonique et Afrique Noire', in *Revue Historique*, April–June 1962, p. 329.
6 Lucy Mair, *Primitive Government*, London, 1962, p. 15.
7 G. W. B. Huntingford, 'The Peopling of the Interior of East Africa by its Modern Inhabitants' in *History of East Africa* (ed. R. Oliver and G. Mathew), Oxford, 1963, p. 66.
8 See for example J. Goody, 'Feudalism in Africa?' in *The Journal of African History*, 1963, No. 1.
9 In R. S. Rattray, *Ashanti Law and Constitution*, Oxford, 1929, p. 82.
10 Mair, op.cit., p. 39.
11 J. C. Anene in the *Journal of the Historical Society of Nigeria*, December 1961, p. 289.
12 G. Fortune, 'The Contribution of Linguistics to Ethnohistory' in the *Proceedings* of the Tropical Africa History Conference of September 1960, Salisbury, 1962, p. 17.
13 J. Greenberg, 'Langues et histoire en Afrique' in *Présence Africaine*, 1963, No. 1, p. 35.
14 Audrey I. Richards, 'The Political System of the Bemba Tribe' in *African Political Systems* (ed. M. Fortes and E. E. Evans-Pritchard), Oxford, 1940, p. 82.
15 T. Olawale Elias, *The Nature of African Customary Law*, Manchester, 1956, p. 162.
16 *Ntu*, 3 Collingham Gardens, London, S.W.5., January 1962.
17 In G. Stinglhamber and P. Dresse, *Léopold II au travail*, Brussels,

1945, p. 52; quoted in Jean Stengers, 'Études historiques', *Tome* 1 *du Livre Blanc de l'Académie Royale etc.*, Brussels, 1962, p. 125.

18 G. S. P. Freeman-Grenville, 'The German Sphere 1884–98' in *History of East Africa*, p. 444.

19 In Basil Davidson, *Report on Southern Africa*, London, 1962, p. 62.

20 In *Report of Central African Council* (Migrant Labour), Salisbury, 1947.

21 In Basil Davidson, *The African Awakening*, London, 1955, p. 204.

22 *Colonial Students in Britain*, Political and Economic Planning, London, 1955, p. 55.

23 In Davidson, op. cit., p. 236.

24 *The Educated African*, ed. R. Sloan and H. Kitchen, London, 1962.

25 In Christopher Fyfe, *A History of Sierra Leone*, Oxford, 1962, p. 87.

26 In David Kimble, *A Political History of Ghana*, Oxford, 1963, p. 545.

27 op. cit., p. 537.

28 R. C. Haw, *No Other Home*, Bulawayo, 1962, p. 7.

29 Adriano Moreira, *Portugal's Stand in Africa*, New York, 1962, p. vi.

30 In G. Shepperson and T. Price, *Independent African*, Edinburgh, 1958, p. 163.

31 Mentioned by T. O. Ranger in the introduction to *Proceedings* of the Tropical Africa History Conference, 1960, *supra*.

32 In Fritz-Ferdinand Müller, *Deutschland-Zanzibar-Ostafrika*, Berlin, 1959, p. 455, drawing on archives of Reichskolonialamt, Deutschen Zentralarchiv, Potsdam.

33 Petöfi Sándor: *Eszkesünk, eszkesünk,*
                 Rovák tovább nem leszünk !

34 Ndabaningi Sithole, *African Nationalism*, Oxford, 1959, p. 100.

35 Sir A. B. Ellis, *The Ewe-Speaking Peoples of the Slave Coast of West Africa*, London, 1890, p. 9.

36 J. Mensah Sarbah, *The Fanti Constitution*, London, 1906, in Kimble, op. cit., p. 540.

37 J. E. Caseley Hayford, *West African Leadership* (collected speeches), Stockwell, 1949.

38 Martin R. Delany, *The Condition, Elevation, Emigration, and Destiny of the Colored People of the United States, Politically Considered*, Philadelphia, 1852, p. 210, in G. Shepperson, 'Notes on Negro American Influences on the Emergence of African Nationalism' in the *Journal of African History*, 1960, No. 2, p. 299.

39 Sithole, op. cit., p. 20.

40 In Thomas Hodgkin, 'A note on the Language of African Nationalism', *St Anthony's Papers*, No. 10 (ed. Kenneth Kirkwood), London, 1961, p. 24.

41 loc. cit., p. 25.

42 In Colin Legum, *Pan-Africanism*, London, 1962, p. 15.

43 In *Spark*, Accra, 26 April 1963.

44 See especially Shepperson and Price, op. cit.

45 In Legum, op. cit., p. 28.

46 Summarized by Legum, p. 133.

47 Kwame Nkrumah, *Africa Must Unite*, London, 1963, p. 141.

48 op. cit., p. 142.

49 *Daily Express*, 14 January 1960.

50 In Kimble, p. 548.

51 Translated by Marjorie Grene in Janheinz Jahn, *Muntu*, London, 1961, p. 238.

52 In Ezekiel Mphahlele, *The African Image*, London, 1962, p. 26.

53 loc. cit., p. 27.

54 In Langston Hughes, *An African Treasury*, London, 1961, p. 185.

55 In Basil Davidson, 'The African Personality', *Africa, A Handbook* (ed. Colin Legum), London, 1961, p. 450.

56 In *Black Mother*, translation by Basil Davidson, London, 1961, p. 233. Original in M. de Andrade, *Antologia*, Paris 1958.

57 Ulli Beier, *Art in Nigeria 1960*, Cambridge, 1960, p. 9.

58 Mphahlele, op. cit., p. 24.

59 In Keatley, op. cit., p. 222.

60 Haw, op. cit., p. 1.

61 Geoffrey Parrinder, *West African Religion*, London, 1961, 9. p.

62 Placide Tempels, *La Philosophie bantou*, Paris, 1948, p. 112.

63 *Ntu* editorials, London, 1962.

64 Margaret Field, *Search for Security*, London, 1960, p. 29.

65 In Jack Woddis, *The Roots of Revolt*, London, 1960, p. 30.

66 In Davidson, *Report on Southern Africa*, p. 62.

67 ibid., p. 66.

68 *Report* of the East Africa Royal Commission 1953–5, Cmd. 9475, p. 37.

69 In Marvin Harris, *Portugal's African 'Wards'*, New York, 1958, p. 33.

70 L. Marquet in the *Bulletin* of the Centre d'Études des Problèmes Sociaux Indigènes, Elisabethville, 1946, No. 2, p. 16.

71 In Davidson, *Report on Southern Africa*, p. 98.

72 ibid., p. 93.

73 C. W. de Kiewiet, *A History of South Africa*, Oxford, 1941, p. 161.

74 *Voice of Africa*, Accra, 6 March 1963.

75 Report of Debates, Legistive Assembly, Salisbury, 30 November 1944.

76 B. Gussman in Woddis, op. cit., p. 140.

77 ibid., p. 234.

78 *Report* of the East Africa Royal Commission, pp. 45 and 206.

79 In Woddis, ibid., p. 209.

80 Quoted by E. Dhanis in *Zaire*, May 1953, p. 489.

81 K. A. Busia, *A Report on a Social Survey of Sekondi-Takoradi*, Crown Agents, 1950, p. 93.

82 Georges Balandier, 'Sociological Survey of the African Town of Brazzaville' in *Social Implications of Industrialization etc. ... South of the Sahara*, UNESCO for International African Institute, 1956, p. 108.

83 *Report* of the East Africa Royal Commission, p. 50.

84 ibid., p. 214.

85 N. de Cleene, *Le Clan matrilinéal dans la société indigène*, Inst. Roy. Col. Belge, 1946, p. 70.

86 In Conor Cruise O'Brien, *To Katanga and Back*, London, 1962, p. 84, footnote.

87 O'Brien, p. 238.

88 U.N. Mission *Report on Ruanda Urundi*, 1960, vol. 1, p. 131.

89 Ayo Ogunsheye, 'Whither West Africa?', *Listener*, 8 October 1959.

90 *Flash*, Durban, 11 November 1952.

91 Thomas Hodgkin and Ruth Schachter, *French-Speaking West Africa in Transition*, Carnegie Endowment, May 1960, p. 405.

92 In Davidson, *The African Awakening*, p. 135.

93 René Dumont, *L'Afrique noire est mal partie*, Paris, 1962, p. 34.

94 G. M. Carstairs, *This Island Now* (B.B.C. Reith Lectures), London, 1963, p. 55.

95 André Blanchet: in Gwendolen M. Carter (ed.) *African One-Party States*, New York, 1962, p. 275.

96 Margery Perham, 'Britain and Africa in 1963', *Listener*, 4 April 1963.

97 Julius K. Nyerere, *Democracy and the Party System*, Dar-es-Salaam, 1963, p. 15.

98 In *Spark*, Accra, 15 March 1963.

99 Nyerere, *Democracy and the Party System*, p. 15.

100 Lord Hailey, *Native Administration in the British African Territories*, London, H.M.S.O., 1951, part 4, page 2.

101 In G. M. Childs, *Umbundu Kinship and Character*, London, 1949, p. 23.

102 Rattray, op. cit., p. 82.

103 Field, op. cit., p. 26.

104 See, for example, Sithole, op. cit., p. 97.
105 Senator A. J. Ellender quoted in *Africa Today*, New York, May 1963, p. 4.
106 R. N. Donaldson, 'Tanganyika's Economy', *Venture*, London, January 1960, p. 5.
107 Kimble, op. cit., p. 22.
108 See especially Nkrumah, *Building a Socialist State*, Accra, 1961.
109 Kwame Nkrumah, *Autobiography*, London, 1957, appendix A.
110 Hodgkin and Schachter, op. cit., p. 387.
111 Julius K. Nyerere, '*Ujamaa*': *The Basis of African Socialism*, Dar es Salaam, 1962, p. 3.
112 J. S. Kasambala, statement at opening of All-African Conference on Cooperatives, Moshi, November 1962.
113 Mamadou Dia, *The African Nations and World Solidarity* (trans. Mercer Cook), London, 1962, p. 29.
114 Alhaji Sir Ahmadu Bello, Sardauna of Sokoto, *My Life*, in *West Africa*, 1 December 1962.
115 Kwame Nkrumah, *Sunday Times*, 9 January 1960.
116 Kwame Nkrumah, *Africa Must Unite*, London, 1963, p. 173.
117 Sékou Touré, *La Planification économique*, Conakry, 1960, p. 77.
118 Guy Hunter, *The New Societies of Tropical Africa*, Oxford, 1962, p. 186.
119 Woddis, op. cit., p. 227.
120 *Memorandum on Mining in the Gold Coast*, Government Printing Department, Accra (marked *Confidential, Limited Circulation*), 1951, esp. p. 25.
121 *Central Africa in Business*, Voice and Vision Ltd, 1962, p. 18.
122 In Davidson, *Tomorrow's Africa*, London, 1962, p. 8.
123 *Frankfurter Allgemeine Zeitung*, 12 September 1958.
124 *Die Welt*, 14 March 1959.
125 *Der Spiegel*, 7 February 1962.
126 In Davidson, 'Jacobins in Africa', *History Today*, February 1959.
127 *Daily Mail*, 12 June 1963.
128 Dumont, op. cit., p. 70.
129 ibid., p. 65.
130 *Report of the Coker Commission of Inquiry into the Affairs of Certain Statutory Corporations in Western Nigeria*, Federal Ministry of Information, Lagos, 1962, vol. 1, p. 37.
131 ibid., p. 3.
132 *Révolution Africaine*, Algiers, No. 1, 2 February 1963.
133 Tom Stacey, *Sunday Times*, 19 May 1963.
134 Dumont, op. cit., p. 119.
135 Colin Legum (ed.), *Africa Handbook*, p. 234.

136 *Tunisia Works*, Secretariat of State for Information, Tunis, 1960, p. 130.

137 Anouar Abdel-Malek, *Égypte, société militaire*, Paris, 1962, p. 75.

138 In André Mandouze, *La Révolution algérienne par les textes*, Paris, 1961, p. 126.

139 ibid., p. 115.

140 *El Moudjahid*, 21 December 1961.

141 Figures given to me by Si Abdulazziz, Director of the Office National de la Réforme Agraire, Algiers, in October 1963.

142 H. L. Bretton, *Power and Stability in Nigeria*, New York, 1963, quoted in *West Africa*, 23 March 1963.

143 Sir Ahmadu Bello, Sardauna of Sokoto, *My Life*, in *West Africa*, 17 November 1962.

144 Tai Solarin, 'A View of Nigerian Independence', in *African Independence* (ed. Peter Judd), New York, 1963, p. 246.

145 *West Africa* editorial, 23 March 1963.

146 *The Economic Development of Nigeria*, Report of a Mission Organized by the International Bank for Reconstruction and Development, Baltimore and Oxford, 1955, p. 14.

147 *Economic Rehabilitation of Eastern Nigeria*, Report of the Economic Mission to Europe and North America, Government Printer, Enugu, 1955, p. 4.

148 *West Africa*, 7 April 1962.

149 James Mossman in 'Panorama', 16 May 1963.

150 *Time*, 3 August 1962.

151 *Atlantic Monthly*, November 1962.

152 Dunduza K. Chisiza, *Africa – What Lies Ahead*, New York, 1962, p. 28.

153 Nkrumah, *Africa Must Unite*, p. 54.

154 *The Times*, 8 May 1963.

155 Nkrumah, *Building a Socialist State:* speech of 22 April 1961.

156 F. M. Bourret, *The Gold Coast*, Oxford, 1949, p. 135.

157 Nkrumah, *Daily Graphic* (Accra), 26 March 1963.

158 Walter Schwarz, *Daily Graphic*, 5 March 1962.

159 Nkrumah, speech of 24 March 1962.

160 loc. cit.

161 M. A. Ribeiro, *Daily Graphic*, 1 July 1963.

162 *Daily Graphic*, 1 July 1963.

163 Jacques Charrière, 'Une Expérience de planification', *Cahiers internationaux*, Paris, March–April 1961, p. 82.

164 J. M. Kariuki, '*Mau Mau*' *Detainee*, with a foreword by Margery Perham, Oxford, 1963, p. 181.

165 Bello, *My Life*, in *West Africa*, 24 November 1962.

166 Madéira Kéita, 'Democracy and the One-Party State', *Fighting Talk*, March 1962.

167 *Report of the Nyasaland Commission of Inquiry.* Cmd. 814, 1959.

168 *Observer*, 8 October 1961.

169 *Guardian*, 27 May 1963.

170 Kariuki and Perham, pp. 137 and xii respectively.

171 *Reporter*, Nairobi, 11 April 1963.

172 E. H. Carr, 'The Russian Revolution and the Peasant', *Listener*, 30 May 1963 (abridgement of British Academy Raleigh Lecture, 1963).

173 *Observer*, 2 January 1963.

Index

*Other volumes in the Penguin African Library
are described on the following pages*

A Short History of Africa

Roland Oliver and J. D. Fage

For some years now there has been an urgent need for a concise history of Africa. Although much has been written on different regions of Africa and different periods of her long development – colonial histories of the European powers, current affairs articles on the emergent countries, studies of Africa's prehistory – there has been nothing that offers the general reader an overall view of African history from the earliest times to the Pan-African meetings at Monrovia and Casablanca.

Drawing on archaeology, oral tradition, language relationships, social institutions, and material cultures, the Editors of the *Journal of African History* present *A Short History of Africa* which not only assembles the most authoritative views of their colleagues into an absorbing narrative, but also contains some original conclusions that take the study of Africa a stage farther.

African Profiles

Ronald Segal

This is not only a handy reference book of information on Africa's leading personalities but, at the same time, a readable outline of the history and political structure of all but a handful of minor territories. In short it is the intelligent man's guide to the African continent.

Ronald Segal, whose *Political Africa* quickly established itself as a vital work of reference, here provides an indexed background against which we can evaluate the flood of news coming from Africa. The need for emancipation and unity, which is his basic theme, is supported by detailed analyses of many crucial issues – the crisis in the Congo, Portugal's African empire, the Central African Federation, and *apartheid* in South Africa. In addition the author makes assessments of Nasser's socialism, Nkrumah's experiments in African leadership, federalism in East Africa, the throne of Morocco, military rule in the Sudan, and democracy in Nigeria.

Portugal in Africa

James Duffy

Everyone knows that Portugal is 'Britain's oldest Ally', but that is precisely where for most of us our knowledge both begins and ends. Although the recent crisis in Angola focused world attention on Portugal's African colonies, all too little was known about either the immediate causes of conflict or the wider issue of Portugal's long rule in Africa.

This is the first book to offer the general reader an authoritative and detailed study of Portugal in Africa. It is a fascinating story of *praziero* and *soba*, missionary and explorer, *assimilado* and slave, of brilliant promise and squalid achievement.

The procession of explorers, governors, chiefs, and slave-traders takes the reader from the first fingers of exploration in the fifteenth century to the final façade of the Salazar régime and shows how the crescendo of imperial delusion, set against the brutal reality of five centuries of exploitation, led at last to the bloodshed of Angola.

Portuguese Africa borders on the Congo, South West Africa, and the Central African Federation. The historical experience which Mr Duffy relates is therefore of the greatest importance not only for Angola and Moçambique but for the future of Africa as a whole.

South West Africa
Ruth First

South West Africa has recently stepped into the news and may any day seize the headlines. This book, by a well-known South African journalist, is the first concise yet comprehensive survey of the reasons why South West Africa is today one of the most vital areas of the African continent.

Ruth First traces the course of over eighty years' economic and political exploitation of the African population by a succession of white powers, from the original British and Dutch traders to the Nationalist régime begun in 1948. She shows how the African majority has been progressively deprived of lands, political representation, and the means of full economic development. But she argues also that the ironic tragedy whereby a League of Nations mandate became an instrument of oppression may yet become a source of hope. The U.N. Trusteeship Committee, the International Court of Justice, and South West Africa's shared frontiers with Angola, Northern Rhodesia, and Bechuanaland may help the territory and turn it into the Achilles' heel of *apartheid.*

East Africa: The Search for Unity
Kenya, Tanganyika, Uganda, and Zanzibar

A. J. Hughes

For two generations the climate, scenery, and sporting life of Kenya have attracted a stream of wealthy white settlers – pioneers who peopled the White Highlands, planted new crops, opened mines, helped to officer the King's African Rifles, and silently to their surprise generated the native opposition which culminated a few years ago in the Mau Mau insurrection.

Today we see Kenya committed to the principle of federation with Tanganyika, Uganda, and Zanzibar – neighbours with very different histories. Such an imaginative experiment could have the profoundest consequences for the whole of Africa. Nyasaland and Northern Rhodesia might be drawn into the orbit of such a force, which could well set the political style for the rest of the continent.

The author of *East Africa* has spent several years as a political correspondent in East Africa and as an official of one of the nationalist parties. In his account of the histories of these diverse countries he underlines the boldness of this political venture. Whilst Kenya was a British colony, Uganda was made a Protectorate – an area of indirect government – in 1890. Zanzibar, like the coastal ports of the mainland, is largely Arabic in character, and Tanganyika, before the Mandate, was German territory.

This is the first full survey in one volume of the histories and politics of this part of Africa. It graphically outlines a brave and crucial political experiment.

The Rise of the South African Reich

Brian Bunting

This, as its title implies, is an analysis of the drift towards Fascism of the white government of the South African Republic. It documents the close affinities of thought and action between such men as Malan, Strijdom, Verwoerd, and Vorster and the German Nazi leaders, and traces the contact maintained by the Nationalist Party with Nazis during the last thirty years.

It is a revelation to read how faithfully, in the wartime draft Constitution, Malan aped Hitler, and how – spurred perhaps by that secret sinister organization, the Broederbond – that Nationalist Party has, one by one, enacted its tyrannous measures. Racial laws, censorship, control of Trade Unions, an 'Iron and Blood' re-armament programme, manipulation of state capital, elimination of opposition, and mass indoctrination through such agencies as Christian National Education – these are now established features of South Africa.

Many of the documents quoted by Brian Bunting in this book will undoubtedly shock and horrify thousands of readers.

PB 21738
2

For a complete list of books available please write to Penguin Books whose address can be found on the back of the title page